The
Art Studio/Loft
Manual

For Ambitious Artists and Creators

Eric Rudd

CIRE
CORPORATION
P U B L I S H E R

North Adams, Massachusetts

The Art Studio/Loft Manual
for Ambitious Artists and Creators
Eric Rudd

CIRE Corporation - Publisher
An imprint of Cire Corporation
Historic Beaver Mill
189 Beaver Street
North Adams, MA 01247-2873 USA
Orders and information:order@cirepub.com, www.cirepub.com
or (800) 689-0978

Copyright © 2001 by Eric Rudd
First Printing 2001

Printed by Proforma Universal Marketing, North Adams, MA

Cover Design by Keith Bona; photograph courtesy of MASS MoCA

Publisher's Cataloging-in-Publication Data
(Provided by Quality Books, Inc.)

Rudd, Eric.
    The art studio/loft manual : for ambitious artists and creators/Eric Rudd. −1st ed.

    p. cm.
    Includes index.
    LCCN: 2001089008
    ISBN: 0-9709959-1-1

1. Artists' studios. 2. Artists—Housing. 3. Real property. 4. Buildings—Remodeling for other use.
I. Title.

N8520.R83 2001   700'.68'2
                                         QB101-200630

Contents

About the Author
Acknowledgements
Note to the Reader
Disclaimer

Introduction

1 **About Studio/Loft Spaces** 13
   Available Space
   New York?
   Space Needs
   How Big?
   Types of Studios

2 **Real-Estate Matters** 39
   How to Look
   Location
   Rent or Mortgage?
   Negotiation
   Purchase Contracts
   Before Settlement
   Warning Checklist

3 **Money Matters** 83
   Financing
   Loan Amortization
   Lowering the Payment
   Money Sources

4 **Legal Matters** 95
   Legal Ownership
   Renting to Others
   Commercial Leases
   Problems with Tenants

5 **Design & Planning** 109
   Best Use
   Design Basics
   Paper, Computer, Actual

6 Construction **121**
Priorities
Suppliers
Permits and Inspections
Roof, Electrical, Plumbing,
Lighting, Sprinklers, Alarms
Walls, Floors, Ceilings
Hazardous Wastes
Code Issues

7 Building Materials **157**
Wall Systems
Light Systems
New Materials

8 Equipment & Function **169**
Studio Sections
Tools
Functional Areas

9 Operational Expenses **179**
Save on Monthly Expenses
Administrative Techniques
Energy Programs

10 Loft Living as an Accessory Use **195**
Considerations
Building Components

11 Artists' Buildings & Organizations **205**
Artists' Group Buildings
Committees
Positives and Negatives
Residency Facilities
Not-for-Profits
Public Funds
Long-Term Ideas

Summary **227**
Taking Stock

Sample Commercial Lease
Sample Letter to Tenant
Index
Order Forms

Preface – Note to the Reader

There has been no survey to my knowledge counting the number of artists and creators working in studios. Numbers are easily tossed around. Some estimates indicate that several hundred thousand visual artists are working in New York City alone. How many are working in spare bedrooms and how many rent separate studios or live in studio/lofts is anyone's guess.

There are probably half a million serious visual artists in this country, and that is a conservative estimate. You must at least triple that number if you count dancers, musicians, performers, filmmakers, craftspeople and other creators. To practice their art, most of these creators use studios - either by renting, purchasing, or sharing large working spaces.

With thousands of spaces being used, and almost all on a very limited budget, the needs are great. I have not found another book that gives realistic, practical advice on how to secure a good working space.

Disclaimer:

This book is an attempt to outline most of the issues involved with studio spaces. Many lessons have been learned the hard way. However, with hundreds of thousands of space possibilities, there is not room to go through every contingency. The author, while experienced, is not a lawyer, accountant, licensed contractor or other licensed expert.

The purpose of this book is to introduce ideas and issues. You are responsible for seeking expert advice about all individual cases. The author and the publisher shall have neither liability nor responsibility to any person or entity with respect to any loss or damage caused, or alleged to have been caused, directly or indirectly, by the information contained in this book.

If you do not wish to be bound by the above, before continuing, you may return this book to the publisher for a full refund.

Acknowledgements:

In one book, I cannot acknowledge all the people who have given me advice throughout my career and who helped and advised me with each studio, house or industrial property that I've moved into.

Foremost thanks go to my wife, Barbara, who has shared in the struggle and rewards. She has been an active partner in all of this.

I want to thank my sons Thaddeus and Nikolai, now grown, but who grew up with various art experiences and visited many studios.

The real thanks should go to all the carpenters, plumbers, electricians, sheetrock hangers, and other tradespeople who have put their time and knowledge to work. Names like Sonny, Harry, Van, Tim, Armand, Jim, Ralph and others bring back vivid memories of past building projects.

Equal thanks go to the bankers, lawyers, accountants, real-estate developers, building owners, architects and others whom I've pushed into the brand-new world of dealing with artists; I hope they enjoyed it, because, believe me, the monetary rewards were slim.

Thanks go also to all the artists with whom I've been in contact over the years; all have put their vision into making studio spaces come alive.

Finally I want to acknowledge the people who helped to put this book into final form- Keith Bona for design, Mary Misch, Ulrica Rudd and Barbara Rudd for editing, the North Adams Transcript, Caroline Bonnivier and MASS MoCA for photos, and Joe Manning for making an important early suggestion.

Dedicated
To Barbara

About The Author

Eric Rudd is a well-known sculptor/mixed media artist. He has exhibited extensively for thirty-five years and is represented in many museums and private collections. His exhibition, the *Dark Ride Project* (www.darkrideproject.org), is a futuristic 15,000-square-foot art installation that includes an actual ride on the robotic "Sensory Integrator" through "creative space." He is currently working on robotic sculpture installations, an epic installation for "A Chapel for Humanity," and his first "Top Secret" project.

Eric started several art buildings; his current studio – one of the largest individual studios in the country- is located in the 130,000-square-foot, historic Beaver Mill. Eric founded and for ten years directed the Contemporary Artists Center (www.thecac.org), a not-for-profit artists' studio residency and exhibition facility.

Eric has been instrumental in helping several new and alternative galleries and museums; he has worked with many new industrial materials and processes; he has been the recipient of fellowship grants from the National Endowment for the Arts and the Japan Foundation; he has created art during corporate and foreign residencies; and he has taught, lectured and been politically active and idealistic as an artist.

While busy with many art projects, Eric was prompted to write this book because so many artists came to him for advice about securing studio space. Equally compelling is Eric's desire for artists to have better studios in order to carry out their work. We hope his experience and successful examples can work for you.

Eric Rudd is the author of <u>The Art World Dream: Alternative Strategies for Working Artists</u>.

The Art World Dream
Alternative Strategies for Working Artists
(order forms at the end of the book)

Are You an Ambitious Artist?

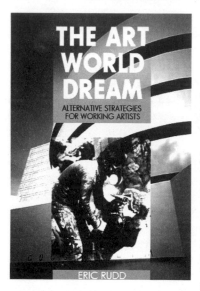

Every artist wants his or her work to hang in the Museum of Modern Art, the Guggenheim, and the Whitney - if not soon, then sometime in the not too distant future. This would signify recognition, financial success and the artist's place in art history.

Whether you are just setting out on a career in art, or have been working for a few years and feel that you can't break free, this book will help you set up your life to allow the art - which you are capable of making - happen. It is not an elementary 'how to paint' or 'how to be an artist' manual. There are plenty of advice books already written for that. That's like giving you advice on how to go hiking in the woods.

You aren't going for a hike; you want to climb Mount Everest! For such an undertaking, there definitely are steps to consider and ways someone can help you. No book can tell you if you will have the strength, but a book can tell you how much strength you will need and how to measure your strength. No book will guarantee that you will be able to raise the funds to finance such an expedition, but a book can tell you what you will probably need and whether there are ways to attain it more easily.

Finally, this book will tell you about other peaks, just as challenging, and present new concepts for you to consider. This book will help you undertake an artistic mission of the most serious nature, needing the utmost determination from you.

Artist Eric Rudd has not only created impressive art that pushes into new technologies, he has also built an incredible infrastructure to do his work. His personal studio complex is inspiring. I would advise other artists to observe what he has done."

Thomas Krens, Director, Solomon R. Guggenheim Museum

A Must-Read for All Serious Artists!

Introduction:

Art studios and lofts come in all shapes and sizes and are used by all sorts of artists and creators. The one thing they have in common is that artists want very large studios and have very modest budgets.

Artists are pioneers. In search of cheap workspace, they often go into run-down neighborhoods and take over unwanted buildings. When the atmosphere of the area or individual property improves, they are driven from these same places when landlords try to cash in and either sell at appreciated prices or simply raise rents. The value of the artist 'taking a chance' is easily forgotten in search of more dollars.

There are better solutions. SoHo studios in the 1960s went for the asking; there were a few smart artists who bought their spaces, which today are worth millions. Even with very limited cash resources, there are options.

Why did I write this manual? For two basic reasons: First, for years, in addition to doing my own work, I've spent a percentage of my time teaching, helping art organizations and helping artists. This book is my payback to help artists find and keep good studios. Second, artists are constantly coming to me for advice in getting good studios. I've always tried to help, but this has added up to a lot of lost time. Now I can suggest that artists should read this manual. It offers much more than I can say in just a few minutes.

I've always been aggressive in seeking large workspaces for myself. While large spaces do not necessarily translate into good work, without adequate space to carry out our creative endeavors, great art won't get made.

All of my studios have been learning experiences. Today, I have one of the largest studios in the country. I have a mill the size of a city block and personally use about a third of it. Plus, I have room to expand.

As a typical artist in earlier years, I found cheap places to rent. Usually, I was able to find incredible deals, but every time I had one, I felt that any occupancy over five years was a bonus. The time between studios was always very stressful. It was not only stressful to look for a new studio with a deadline to vacate my present studio hanging over me, but the actual move and resettling disrupted my creative processes. Finally, it dawned on me to stop moving and wasting time getting newly acclimated, and try to secure permanent space that could carry me many years into the future.

Young artists dream of instant fame. They think studios will be just small side issues. But even fame brings demands for space that can easily break the bank. And the more common state of artists getting some recognizable success will mean that affordable space will be critical in order to carry out further creative work. Income from modest success will still not be rewarding enough to pay for almost any space without budgetary concern.

As I am a painter/sculptor/new media artist, this book will reference visual artists mostly, but people in all fields use studios and lofts. A theater organization would benefit as much as a sculptor from the points made in this book.

You may read this book and feel that, instead of dealing with art, you are dealing with construction and real estate. During a student's studies, most art schools fail to present the realities of living and working as an artist. For a working artist, too often lessons are learned the hard way.

Schools that do address these issues teach antiquated methods, and developing artists have little knowledge of more efficient ways to deal with the business aspects of art. I look forward to the day when art schools carry "Manufacturing Processes and Economics," "Management," and "Real Estate" in their curriculums.

Whether you want to or not, as an artist you will be dealing with all of these issues in one form or another. I would make a pitch that along with this book, you read The Art World Dream: Alternative Strategies for Working Artists. Together, the two books will offer you, the serious artist or creator, a world of new opportunities.

I compare dealing with real estate to a painter building a stretcher, then putting the canvas onto the stretcher and priming it – getting it ready for paint. It really has little to do with the masterpiece that might come out, but it is a necessary infrastructure to allow the painting to be done. If artists had lots of money, then those aspects would be taken care of by others; that's not the usual case.

As I often state, it might be fine to be emotional and splash paint on canvas, but too many artists are walking around with fewer than ten fingers because they did not learn the methods to use, and the attitudes to have, when cutting frames or stretchers on a table saw. Likewise, when I see a good artist being evicted from his/her studio, I wonder if a little effort a few years earlier could have prevented this struggle.

Finally, I want to emphasize that finding, securing, and fixing up a studio takes time. You will start small, but surely, if you are ambitious and dedicated, you will get into larger and larger spaces. The rewards might be enjoyed a few years ahead.

My wife and I founded a not-for-profit artists' studio residency and exhibition facility. Over the course of a decade, I learned that many artists who came to work there had career-altering experiences and breakthroughs. Often, however, this realization didn't come about for at least six months after they returned to their own studios and work.

Keep this in mind as you read, and hopefully re-read, this manual. If it affects you or helps you, I would love to know. Feel free to drop me an e-mail or a note.

Eric Rudd

11

CHAPTER 1
About Studio/Loft Spaces

Artists seek low-rent and not-in-demand areas. It once was easy to be in SoHo; today you couldn't afford a closet there.

A PERSONAL EXPERIENCE

If, after this discussion, you think that I must be thinking all the time about real estate instead of art, I want to assure you that if you could see how much art I've created you would change your mind. I put space as a priority, but only in order to carry out my artistic goals.

It has taken me some years to build up to it, but finally I can smile at it all. I have one of the largest individual art studios in the country. With our loft, I'm using about 60,000 square feet in the historic Beaver Mill, and I can expand easily up to 140,000 square feet. Our loft space has 8,000 square feet; in New York City that would cost several million dollars. (For the first few years, local residents would ask with puzzled expressions, "You live in a factory?") I live in a place where people go to on vacation (five months depend on your attraction to cold weather and skiing, but the other seven months are, without any question, beautiful), and some of the most interesting people in the art world not only come to the Berkshires but now to my mill also. I have all the technical help nearby I could ever need or even get in a large metropolitan area. (I work with industrial equipment and processes – blow-molders, polyurethane spray foam, resins, silicones, airless paint spray, robotics, computers, multi-media, etc.) I am very close to more cultural stimulation than I ever was able to access easily when I lived in Washington, D.C. (Everything is easy to get to, much is free, and never crowded.) Best of all, I am just up the road from one of the most visible contemporary art museum projects in recent years, which has the Guggenheim Museum as one of the

13

participants. If I had ten million dollars in the bank I don't think I could live, as an artist, in a better spot on the globe. If I am making your mouth water, I do it on purpose.

It is important to point out that the accumulation of space, in my case a lot of space, is not directly linked to how good my art is. On the other hand, with this kind of space, I can organize my studio to better implement various processes, store my works and carry out my own large-scale experiments without needing the permission of the art world gurus.

Great studio space is needed in order to develop great art - not only to do work now - but to do work for a long period of time. This means working for the rest of this year, next year, for five years, for ten years, forever. To pay for this space - if you are not famous - will require time and money. Are there systems and strategies to make this happen without just having to be lucky? Read on.

A GLOBAL PERSPECTIVE

After World War II, Europe was the place where artists could go, be inspired by centuries of art, and live as well as work cheaply. American tourists soon became the arrogant symbol of power. As other defeated countries rebuilt their economies, products and materials were cheap by American standards. During this era, when American productivity dominated each industry, American art also dominated the international art market, especially as the nucleus shifted from Paris to New York.

Although America is still the biggest economy and New York is still the biggest art center, there are still plenty of places where cheap labor can be found elsewhere in the world, as economics have changed. Areas of cheap labor are rather remote and changing rapidly. The biggest splash of cold water is the realization that America is no longer the dominating leader in the world; in fact, we are sometimes treated like the third-world nation we used to call others. Go to Asia and Europe, and you will find few bargains. Even in Southeast Asia where labor and factory processes are cheap, finding large studio space is not easy.

While America is the largest, its economy is now dependent upon the world's other economies. While New

York has remained the art commerce center, other cities have grown significantly. All this is reflected in real estate. Today, the richest vein for artists to mine is in our own backyard. America has abandoned buildings all over the country, trash containers full of discarded materials from industries, space to allow big, experimental projects to be realized, and to top it off, America still has the largest art market in the world. If we are living the consumer, disposable lifestyle for the most part, artists as scavengers can take advantage of this and be more productive than their counterparts in other nations.

Imagine working in the tiny spaces of Japan, or selling to collectors who have closet-sized homes. There is still an active Japanese art scene, with corporate lobbies fulfilling an exhibition demand, but the scene is very tight by American standards. In many third-world countries, trash is combed through countless times before the few remaining crumbs are burned or buried. Real estate in Europe is also high- priced. True, the successful do well, but the developing artists struggle more with the raw necessities of making art than do their American counterparts.

All in all, artists living in the United States can count their blessings and take advantage of many opportunities available. While support from grants and sales during the last two decades has eroded significantly, when it comes to the practical needs of making art - space and materials - artists can easily find treasures.

Just as I have found a studio paradise, you should not have to settle for inadequate studio space. I have always been aggressive in finding better, larger and cheaper working spaces than my contemporaries. You, too, can tap into better ideas to improve your studio environment.

WHERE TO SETTLE?

You can't imagine David Smith's steel and stainless steel sculptures being produced in a SoHo loft studio. You wouldn't expect Andy Warhol's commercially inspired and produced work to have originated in a rural studio barn. Ed Kienholz's tableau sculptures seem logically to have their origins in the consumer flea markets of southern California. The surrounding environs as well as the studio structure itself can have tremendous impact on the creative output.

Proximity to other cultural stimuli and technical processes will affect the creative production as well. If you had millions of dollars, it would be possible to assemble the best elements for positively supporting your work. If you needed land but wanted to be near New York's art culture, it would be possible with adequate funds. But reality being what it is, with physical and monetary limitations, artists usually need to forgo some elements that they would normally want to include. However, consideration first has to be given to needs of space, materials, income sources, cultural stimulation or connections, and family or personal concerns as well as alternative strategies and choices - before artists lock into their studio environments.

In basic terms, usually the closer you are located to art commerce, the more expensive the real estate will be, and therefore the smaller the space you are able to afford. While it is more expensive, the closer an artist is to a major educational and commercial business market, the more resources might be directly available. There are ways, however, to get much larger spaces than would at first appear, as well as a greater possibility of getting superb space not too far away from the 'action.'

Being away from the action is no longer a professional death sentence. With the telephone, fax, computer, Internet, overnight delivery companies and wider distribution of industrial services and products, the ability to be in one particular space for the operational end of your studio work matters less than it used to.

Once settled, it is difficult for artists to pack up and move. Studios involving thousands of square feet of storage, equipment, and new projects do not move about without great disruption to the creative process. So the first decision probably will center on what part of the country (or world) to settle in and its general proximity to various types of resources.

A cityscape will include all sorts of buildings, including bowling alleys, residential apartment buildings, motels as well as other commercial and industrial buildings. Plywood covered windows indicate potential use for the arts.

AVAILABLE LOFT SPACE

Each city and region in the United States has affordable spaces. Even with limited financial resources, the possibilities can be endless. In Washington, D.C., where there are few industrial buildings, artists traditionally had second- and third-floor walk-up studios in row houses, above small commercial stores. The long, narrow space influenced the art being made. In New York, Soho's industrial lofts inspired a different kind of 'large' art, with similar enclaves in other major cities. Southern California has more one-story and newer buildings, and the south has a mixture. In Houston, which doesn't have the traditional zoning laws found everywhere else, artists are in all kinds of spaces, from group industrial buildings to residential properties. New England has vacant mills, although few are broken into small spaces with economical rents. Urban areas having a concentration of artists invite group loft buildings; rural areas encourage conversion of barns, garages and open-air use. Although many artists are forced to begin in their apartment living rooms, spare bedrooms or garages, more professional space is usually sort after. Many processes (cutting lumber, spraying paint and fabricating large works) are difficult to do near residential neighbors.

By definition, a 'loft' space is a shell, with minimum interior partitions. Artists need only the basic necessities - a sink, toilet, heat, electricity and light (hopefully some natural light, but certainly not the valued 'north light' and even natural light is not an absolute necessity for today's contemporary processes) - but otherwise raw space.

The bigger and cheaper the better! The closer to home, work or the art scene, the better.

Loft space as just described, obviously, can get very fancy depending on the desires of the artist or, in other cases, by non-artists who like this kind of space aesthetic for living. The influx of 'yuppies' to former art enclaves has generally resulted in the artists having to move out.

Artists seek low-rent and not-in-demand areas. It once was easy to be in SoHo; today you couldn't afford a closet there. Artists often pioneer areas, and by making them arty, soon appreciate the values of the areas, only to be later driven out by higher rents. Certainly the lambs lose out; the wolves recognize what is going on from the beginning and get a piece of the action. Real estate may not be for everyone, but to me, it is the same as learning to stretch canvas or make a sculpture armature. When considering the long term, which idealistically means the ability to continue to do creative work, early ownership has a lot to offer over constant rent payments and rent increases.

Artists are like vultures. We take what others don't want, because it is affordable. Look in your area at what is not doing well; as will be described elsewhere in this book, when companies close down or move up, they often discard materials and equipment and buildings. Vacant buildings become eyesores; they may be gold mines to you. A vacant building is also a bargain compared to new construction.

NEW STUDIO SPACE COSTS

To build a loft space, which is defined in construction as having windows, minimum interior partitions and the basic necessities as just described, the minimum cost for new construction starts around $60 per square foot for a minimum size, and would be more per square foot for small buildings (more, of course, in some areas, but not much cheaper even where the cost of living is low). Multi-story, urban buildings are even more, and $75 would be a more realistic cost per square foot.

This metal building would cost a lot more with interior partitions, insulation, wndows and plumbing. The land would only be affordable in a rural area.

At $60 per square foot, a smallish 1,000 square foot studio – 20 feet by 50 feet in size - would cost at least $60,000. Because of its small size, however, it could easily cost more. A more workable studio having 5,000 square foot at the $60 per square foot rate would cost at least $300,000, and 10,000 square feet would top $600,000. In all cases, land has to be added to the overall cost. To make it livable with a kitchen and full bath, add another $30,000 or more. Compare this with the cost of existing buildings and you will quickly realize that existing buildings are more affordable.

Like old cars, old buildings are slated to be torn down and replaced. Why? Because older buildings have been fully depreciated and their mortgages have been paid off. Also, bringing old buildings up to date, in order to accommodate many workers or new manufacturing processes, is often more expensive than building from scratch. Additionally, Americans do not have the same appreciation for old properties as do Europeans.

Artists do not have the same demands and needs that companies have. Artists can utilize old buildings in ways that other users cannot. A building that was formerly used by dozens of workers may be used by only one, individual artist. This allows old buildings to be economically feasible for artists while putting new construction out of reach. My mill building would cost more than 7.5 million dollars to build today, and the quality would not be as good. The purchase or market value is far less than the replacement value.

FOLLOW THE PACK?

Groups of artists often take over a large building to share expenses. Usually a building is discovered by one artist and, within a short time, others move in. Some buildings have developed more formally, especially in cities where there is a concentration of artists. The problem with some of these artist-dominated buildings is that, even though they seem attractive, most artists still end up with only one to two thousand square feet - at reasonable rents, but certainly not cheap. My advice is to think at least ten times that scale, and if you do, then these shared or jointly developed buildings don't work - unless you get to the building first and set up the deal. Then you can set it up according to your needs.

In most places, zoning and building codes make converting buildings for studio use difficult. If you want to save money by also living in the studio, it really gets difficult.

There are places where no one cares what you do. Don Judd had airport hangars and an army base in rural

Texas as well as a SoHo loft. David Smith had a farm in upstate New York for his many steel sculptures.

Space allows work to be carried out. Peter Voulkos had two large buildings in Oakland and was a landlord for lots of artists in that community. Anselm Kiefer had more than 5,000 square feet in Germany and was once considering 80,000 square feet in the United States. Andy Warhol's "Factory" was indeed an urban manufacturing plant for new art and ideas. Serious artists need space. Whether you need to rent to others or can afford the space through art sales, the ultimate goal is to satisfy your working needs.

NEW YORK?

Even choosing where to locate is important. Most people live in places where they have jobs, go to school, have family, grew up, or have good connections. Few artists have much of a say in where they would like to live. Unless, of course, they want recognition; artists then will migrate to urban art centers. If you want to become a great actor, you go to New York or to Hollywood. You can have a fine and satisfying career in hundreds of smaller communities, but the lead roles, the big money and the important productions will not happen unless you live in one of those two places. The art world is similar, if you want recognition. But unlike performers who need an audience, you can, of course, create art anyplace. "Anyplace" simply might not be where you can achieve recognition easily. Once you achieve recognition, you can also live anyplace without it negatively affecting your career. You will read later how being in an active art market and having a place in a more economically feasible location can both happen simultaneously.

By the very nature of cities, artists tend to settle where there is an active art scene - near other artists, galleries, collectors, museums and jobs. Many artists settle in the secondary markets, where there is still a lot of action and where success might propel them into the New York, i.e., the international, market. Possibilities include Chicago and Los Angeles, followed by San Francisco, Houston, Dallas, Washington, D.C., and Miami; followed by Philadelphia, Boston, Houston and scores of other cities. Many artists make the case that you can more easily make a name in a smaller market, and then be brought to New York with proper introductions. It depends on whether there are some up-and-coming savvy regional curators who are tuned into the New York scene and will opt to recognize and promote you. Even in smaller markets, the competition can be fierce.

New York City's status as being the dominant center of the international art market is not going to vanish overnight. In your professional lifetime, New York will still be a big factor, whether you choose to work there or not.

Even opting to be in a smaller community may not lead to local recognition. It's a sad state of affairs when you dream of national recognition and you can't even become the leading name in a smaller community, because smaller communities have different standards. They may recognize a good regional artist who will be of no interest to the international art world, and ignore the beginnings of a raw but better talent. Local curators should (but seldom do) try to recognize the local talents - ripe for national attention - and then go to New York to promote them. Theoretically, what helps local artists will help the city or region from which that artist comes. Unfortunately, too many curators try to bring in 'big talent' instead.

Because of this, the action will not come to an isolated studio-barn on an Iowa farm; you have to make the trip and make your presence known in whatever place you want to be attached. This may seem logical, but you would be surprised how many artists live in the boondocks and expect to be discovered. Even in a major city like Washington, I knew artists who would have had national reputations had they not remained there.

Decades ago, I chose to turn down offers to move and show in New York City in order to stay idealistic. There is no question that for the most part, while I did the work I wanted to do, showing in a Washington gallery, instead of a New York gallery that would have automatically received national coverage, dramatically reduced my commercial success. You cannot turn back the clock, so a decision about your studio will substantially affect your entire career.

I also mention the so-called 'mistake' of not moving to New York City when I got invitations from the likes of Henry Geldzahler (he coined the word "Pop" as in "Pop Art"), just as I will mention how I mistakenly didn't follow up on an offer to show at the most prestigious New York gallery of them all back in 1971 - because I want you to realize that if I mention alternative strategies, I have faced the magnetic pull and attraction of New York's success and fame. I know how difficult it is to balance between seeking recognition and doing what it takes to produce the art.

Diane Brown, who for many years operated the Diane Brown Gallery in New York City, used to lament that, in order to give an artist a proper studio visit, even if the studio was, for example, located close by in Brooklyn, she would have to leave the gallery, get a taxi which – door to door - might take 45 minutes to get there in traffic, spend up to a couple of hours if she was really looking at the work and learning where the artist was coming from, as well as giving the artist a fair chance (imagine how you would feel if she was visiting your studio and she came and left after only a few minutes), and then get back to the gallery.   By the time she was back at work, she'd spent/wasted half her day. Studio visits, therefore, had to be selective. With dozens of artists appealing to her each week to visit, you can see the difficulties, and why gallery owners are hesitant to look at work or make studio visits. Besides, they have plenty of other work to do; they need to spend time to get more paying clients for the art they are already showing in order to pay their bills.

And that is what happens when you live a short drive away from the galleries. Imagine the difficulties if you live a few hours away. Slides do not suffice. I knew many artists who used to load up a truck with paintings, drive to New York, and either invite the dealer inside the truck, spread the work out on the sidewalk, pull a few works from the truck and take them inside the gallery, or even set up a mini five-hour show in a hotel room and invite the one or two gallery dealers who had indicated an inclination to come after proper introductions and connections were made in advance.   After expending energy and money doing this kind of thing, your idealistic feelings about creating great art begin to evaporate. They just never mentioned in art school that you would have to go 'hawk' your goods like a vacuum cleaner salesperson.

These comments add up to a powerful rationale for moving to New York City. However, the New York of two decades ago is not the New York of today. The commerce is not the same, the accessibility is not the same, the cluster of artists is not the same, the affordability is not the same, the competition is not the same, the quality of life is not the same, and the likely return of investment is not the same. If I made a mistake not moving to New York a few decades ago, it may not be a mistake today. Today, the opposite might be true.

NOT IN NEW YORK

Having outlined reasons to be in New York, I must now tell you that there are other appealing kinds of locations. If your primary goal is to make great art, there are important considerations that enter the equation. If one chooses to emphasize the process of making the art rather than what happens to the art once it is made, many more artists would be taking a cold, hard look at whether living in New York is advantageous.

No matter where an artist locates, however, it is essential that there exist some degree of art commerce. To live far removed from this activity might do more harm than just the obvious financial considerations. Accessibilty to stimulating activities and artistic opportunities must remain high on the list. On the other hand, without the physical art-making plant, the artist can't even get off the ground.

Of the main priorities, first in order is the ability to get ample studio space. Second, it is just as important to have materials, be able to use processes, and deal with the necessities of living (for yourself and for your family). The third main ingredient is to have proper discourse and contact with other artists, dealers, curators and scholars. And the fourth big component is to have access to income, whether employment is related to art or not. Somehow it all has to be paid for.

New York does not make this easy, especially now. In the 1960s you would end up in a SoHo loft; now you are an hour away in a dangerous section of Brooklyn or across the river in New Jersey. Even if you landed right smack in the middle of SoHo, the competition from multitudes of artists would limit your access. Just try to talk with a museum director in New York and you will see how difficult it is to feel involved.

If you go down the list of needs and examine each material you will need to use and find out how much it will cost and how you will get it physically into your studio; if you examine processes that have to be done, such as framing, printing, cutting, metal finishing, equipment repairing, etc., and again find out who can do these things and how much of a notice is needed and what it will cost; and if you then examine how much you will need for your living expenses and how safe your living area will be, considering spouse and children, their schools, the doctor, hospital, recreational activities, and so forth, and don't forget working and commuting - then New York or the New York area may not be the most conducive place to be, or worth what you get in return. Perhaps you should consider alternatives.

WHO NEEDS A STUDIO?

No matter where in the country you decide to work, if you want to make great art, you need sufficient space. What is the demand? Just in the visual arts, there is a vast number, probably easily over half a million artists, who work in some sort of space devoted to their profession, including painters, sculptors, printmakers, photographers, and now new-media artists. Then add to this list related mediums - crafts and support services - such as studios for doing architectural models, illustration, framing, stretcher building; studios for ceramists, weavers, architects, interior designers, fashion designers, furniture designers, and so forth. Even collectors of art want this kind of space. Not only are they attracted to all aspects of the art world, but they also want to permanently display the art in the type of space in which it was originally fabricated.

In the other arts, there are dancers, actors and new- media performers, filmmakers, TV and video producers, just to name a few. Then there are the organizations and groups, such as theater groups, that may also need, in addition to private workspace, rehearsal and performance space open to the public. Other organizations operate to supply residency spaces for performers, artists and writers. Many of these spaces will have galleries as well. Then there are the thousands of independent galleries that seek loft space. Although most of the galleries want ground-floor space, in large cities they have taken space in multi-story buildings.

Then there are businesses that desire this type of aesthetic. Old factories are now fashionable, 'neat' places to work, and desirable for companies hiring people with a heightened sense of their working surroundings and do not want to spend time in a typical office cubicle, and for companies that can afford the extra expense that this type of space requires for transformation. Even if you just work on a computer screen, you might want 1,000 square feet around you of open space, exposed beams and big windows. A new museum based in a former mill complex in North Adams, Massachusetts called MASS MoCA (Massachusetts Museum of Contemporary Art) is using itself as an anchor to rent out commercial space to new Internet and high-tech businesses, much in the same way a large department store helps to fill up a shopping mall. The income from the rentals helps to pay the museum's operational expenses. The space is in high demand, and companies are attracted not only because of the museum, but also because of the designed mixture of old industrial and new high-tech styles.

All these customers wanting the same kind of space as you, the individual artist, cause much of the inventory to be used up before you can get to it. It also inflates the cost of space. In response, artists have to drop to the lowest level to find affordable space. This will mean studio buildings in rougher shape and in less desirable neighborhoods than one might at first want. But that's the nature of the beast, and it just has to be dealt with. Luckily, there is still an abundance of properties all over the country, and in every community.

HOW BIG?

Bigger is better. You don't know what you will be making five years from now, but if you are productive, you will be adding more and more work, tools, projects and headaches to your workload. Even for very successful artists, storage is a problem. I know artists who are famous, yet they rent storage spaces to store their older work. Very few artists in the world sell everything they make. If you don't want to throw out your work, then you need to be realistic about storage needs.

You are trying to be a professional creator and artist. You need sufficient space to carry out all this work. This will not happen in a cramped little studio somewhere on the top floor of a house.

These sculptures need a lot of space. Painters have it easier.

It may be hard for an artist just a year or two out of school to realize this, but for those of you who have been working for five or ten years, you know the demands.

What few artists do, but what more artists should do, is to assess their needs and then project ten to twenty years ahead. While that can be a bit abstract, now is the time to prepare. Think of it as social security, but in this case, artists don't 'retire' at the age of 65. Taking steps now will allow you to continue to work for as long as you want into your future.

Sculptors might need more space than painters. Dancers need to run and jump. Installation artists need the space to set up their components. Filmmakers need distance for cameras and lights. And all creators need room to pace.

Studios are a reflection of the seriousness of your work. Pretend you are a dealer and you have time to see just one artist out of two who are trying to get your attention. You've heard that each of them is young and good; one paints in his/her garage/spare bedroom/basement and the other has a 10,000-square-foot studio in an industrial warehouse. Which artist are you going to go visit? Which artist do you think might have more potential? This might be a flimsy hypothesis, but in the real world, the artist with 10,000 square feet will most likely have the environment where more serious work can be carried out. To me, space is a most important element in making great art and, at the same time, allowing you to be artistically true to yourself. If you have a big studio, even if you paint miniatures, you are painting small because you choose to, not because you simply don't have the space to carry out large works.

It's easy to find the exceptions if you can't find a large studio and you need inspiration that great art can still be carried out in a tiny space. Morris Louis used to paint in his dining room. His wife worked at a nine-to-five job, and he would create his poured stain canvases during the day, and have them rolled up and put away by the time she returned that afternoon. Pollock's famous studio was just twenty by twenty feet. Yes, it's possible to make great paintings in a closet, but after continuous years at it, unless your paintings can roll up or are flying out the door - sold - you won't have space left to stand.

This medium-sized studio of 700+ square feet is already filled. With paints, stretchers, minimum furniture, phone, frames and other supplies, there is still room to do a sizable work on the floor – but not much more, and only one work at a time. This studio has unusually good light with six big windows, wood floor, high ceilings, exposed brick and beams and in-studio sink. With all utilities included, it would rent for $650 in Washington, D.C.

WHAT SPACE DO YOU NEED?

What are an artist's normal needs? Let's take a painter, for example, and for purposes of this example let us assume he/she is not doing a Cornell type of work (although Joseph Cornell's studio was fascinating and far more extensive than his small works would at first indicate). Our painter will need space to work on one or two paintings at a time, and larger space if the paintings are over ten feet. Combined with space for paints and viewing area, this space is already quite large. Then there is need for table space to do drawings or small works on paper, as well as space for storage of new paper, storage of old drawings, and storage of small and large paintings in a way that paintings can be taken out and be looked at. Also needed is a clean space to frame, assemble stretchers and stretch canvas, or to put protective plastic over the finished paintings. Space for storing the wood for stretchers and frames, and possibly a woodshop area, space for additional supplies, an office/computer area, sink, bathroom, wall to photograph against, and if the artist is into making another type of art, like printmaking, then space for its equipment and supplies is needed as well. For mixed-media artists and sculptors, space needs are multiplied. (Sculptures needing interior installations do not sell or store as easily as sculptures that can go outdoors; no sculptures store as easily as flat canvases.) The idea that I am trying to convey is that all this activity is not going to be professionally carried out in a spare bedroom.

It is also a mindset. You go to your studio, which is very serious and which is obviously set up for the making of great art. You know you are not working in an environment like that of every art hobbyist in the country. This fact alone defines who you are, what you want and how serious you are. The studio is also your work of art. It reflects your explorations, your dreams, your struggles and your diversions.

TYPES OF STUDIOS

It's a big country, and even just considering visual artists, different mediums demand different spaces. There might be more than half a million serious artists working in some sort of studios. Add to that mix, all other kinds of creative work being done by individuals in related fields, and you will see how large of an issue proper studio space is.

New York City Lofts. The most common (and romantic) picture when someone says studio/loft is a walk up, New York City SoHo loft. Sometimes, with luck, there will be a working freight elevator to help carry large works up and down. Otherwise, it's either twisting around staircases or lowering art out the window with rope, hoping no inspector happens by. New York industrial spaces might have clean floors if passed on by former sewing operations, or heavy layers of glue that now need to be stripped in lofts previously used by different manufacturers.

Forty years ago, SoHo studios were cheap. Now, SoHo is for the lawyer who is a partner in a law firm, and the loft may cost several million dollars – for space that might still need hundreds of thousands of dollars in renovation. Where are the artists? Cramped into little studios in buildings with narrow hallways, or in slightly bigger but still small studios - way out in Brooklyn, Jersey City, or Queens, and perhaps in a dangerous area of town.

All big cities have lofts, but they are getting more and more expensive. Nevertheless, among the many multi-story, turn-of-the-century buildings with "New York City-style lofts,' there might be some that are bargains. New York City (Manhattan) is perhaps the only place where the 'bargains' are probably too high for individual artists to buy.

Mills. From a bygone age, and especially in New England, there are vacant mill buildings. Industry moved south, then overseas. These large 'red elephants,' as they are referred to, are not suitable for modern industry needing one-floor, low-utility formats in low-paying and non-union regions of the world.

In eastern Pennsylvania, I looked at mills that really told a sad tale. Once these thriving mills employed entire towns; now they were vacant, and unemployment rates and social services needs were very high. In the middle of one town, I was shown a small mill building of 30,000 square feet. It was unusually clean inside; you could almost have eaten off the floor. I could have bought it for $30,000. All around were modest houses that, if there were a market at all, would sell for more than this building, which was many times their size. The town was only about ninety minutes outside of New York City, so the idea of working there and having access to the city was attractive.

In North Adams, Massachusetts, which you will hear much more about, a 110,000-square-foot mill was sold just three years ago for $100,000. (I will remind you often to re-read the section about square footage and to make sure you know how big this is; an entire football field is about 50,000 square feet.) One dollar a foot is very cheap for rent - but this was for a sale!

Industrial Buildings. All over the country, there are industrial buildings. Manufacturers used to be everywhere; many of their facilities still stand. Look around and don't take a narrow approach. Cheap industrial property can be with land in the outskirts of town, or located right on Main Street. In fact, most areas of the country have struggling neighborhoods. Businesses have moved away from the downtowns to outlying suburban malls. Drive to any small city and see where the Wal-Marts, movie theaters, Gap and Banana Republic stores, Holiday or Comfort Inns and McDonald's, Olive Gardens or other chain eateries have all moved.

Industry also has moved to the outskirts, needing more land, better access to the interstates, and one-story operations. Left abandoned are the multi-story, wood and brick buildings in town.

Commercial Buildings. There are as many large, empty commercial buildings as industrial buildings. They come in all forms - from gas stations to bowling alleys; from office buildings to car dealerships; from five-and-dime stores to abandoned motels; from lumberyards to movie theaters, churches and schools. Anything that once was active and needed large space can now be part of the inventory for artists to consider. For example, I purchased a 9,000-square-foot church three blocks from a museum, and just steps from Main Street. It could serve as a studio with living loft, exhibition space or performance space. Can you imagine how happy a dancer would be? Not many businesses can take these spaces without spending a lot of money to convert them. Artists can often use them 'as is.'

This brick church had two major roof leaks and bricks were falling out. It would not have lasted through another winter. The actual work to save the structure was not that expensive; it only needed immediate work that the previous owner refused to do.

If rural properties have heat, electric and plumbing, they can make ideal working spaces.

Farms. Sculptor David Smith could never have welded his pieces in a New York City loft. Farms have all kinds of traditional barns and newer 'Butler' style metal buildings. Land is cheaper, and an artist can spread out. Obviously, the disadvantage is that culture won't be nearby. But from a point of view of examining the physical resources available, for many artists, farms and related rural buildings should be included for consideration.

The historic Beaver Mill in North Adams, Massachusetts, three hours north of New York City. It has 130,000 square feet, backs up to a state park, and is located in the same town as MASS MoCA (Massachusetts Museum of Contemporary Art.) It is home to the author, fifteen large, private art studios, and the Contemporary Artists Center, a studio residency and exhibition facility.

Residential. Artists do industrial work, but most communities do not have a zoning classification for artwork. For many bureaucrats, artwork means a small canvas on an easel done in a spare bedroom by a hobbyist. But be careful if you move a studio operation into a residential neighborhood. You don't want neighbors to complain and make you move. All kinds of houses can be used for studios, especially if you think of them without any actual living going on. One bedroom could be a woodshop, another a drawing studio, the living room the main studio workplace. Rauschenberg bought up houses on Captiva Island, Florida, for example. I've always had the notion that artists could take some houses in need of repair, strip them down like doing a renovation, but, instead of putting in all the trim, floor and wall covering and finish work, just leave the rooms with sheetrock.

Then when the artist decides to move, the house could be 'finished' and sold. I know an artist who bought two adjacent, very rough row houses (three-story plus basement, both bought for $15,000) in a bad neighborhood. He carved out a living space in one house and used the remaining space and the next-door house for studios. Many years later he was able to cash in on the appreciation. The neighborhood is now trendy.

Take a poor neighborhood and add houses needing a lot of renovation work just to make them livable, and you will find a situation ripe for artists.

Bigger Buildings. Apartment buildings, office buildings, hotels, movie theaters: although I've just mentioned these types of buildings, I bring them up again because I want you to think larger. For the same reason that a run-down house is not easy to sell in a bad neighborhood, an apartment building is worse. But if you think in alternative terms, as for arts uses, you can acquire a lot of space for less. If you think of artists' buildings where you bring in others (which is discussed later), you can leverage resources and make out like a bandit.

Prior to becoming a Holiday Inn, this hotel - with 110 furnished rooms, interior swimming pool and full restaurant - sold at auction for $235,000.

There are buildings and eras to watch for. In Houston, during the 1980s, you could have picked up entire, vacant office buildings. Read the financial papers and follow the commerce of your area. If movie chains are opening up multi-plexes in the malls, look at the old single-screen theaters in town. (Currently, many of those mega-screens are going down the tubes, and perhaps they would be ripe for takeover by live theater groups.) Almost always, newer structures mean that mortgages are still active, and a bank, which will accept a loss on a bad loan, probably will not accept a complete loss. Older properties that have long been paid for can be had for whatever the owner will take, with no bank consideration.

Don't ever think that a property is too large, only that it needs to be analyzed. I never thought I would own, with my resources, a building almost the size of a city block, of which 95% is used for the arts!

Small Towns. There are so many struggling small towns in America they are worth special consideration. A few small towns have special circumstances that make them affluent, but for many, as the shopping malls and Wal-Marts have sucked retail businesses away, the remaining infrastructures are declining.

Towns should be considered like neighborhoods, only with a stronger support network. Towns are desperate to see unwanted buildings be put back to good use. Before individual properties are even considered, you should study the pulse of the town. If you first select a town that will give you proper access to culture, processes and employment, there should be an ample supply of specific properties within the jurisdiction.

All artists should make a pilgrimage to Marfa, Texas, where Don Judd, with financial help from the DIA Foundation, bought up half of the town. Even though it is very remote, it nevertheless is the premier example of setting up a physical infrastructure that is aggressive, independent and successful, all at once. Judd also maintained a SoHo studio/loft.

As I too have discovered, you can become a powerful force in a small community with a reasonable budget. As new aspects of physical space are discussed later in the book, think about alternatives.

Studio/Loft Combos. No matter what type of space is found for a studio, there is a desire and an economic need to combine it with living. Often living runs into building code conflicts when done in industrial buildings, so artists live 'quietly' without permission from the local authorities. A few enlightened cities have passed 'loft laws' to allow artists to live in their studios as an accessory use. Often well-intentioned laws cause more complications. Either the new laws are unclear and make actual use impossible, or the new laws demand so many improvements by the owner that the 'artist' market cannot afford the rents to pay for these improvements and so they never get used by the intended receivers – the serious, struggling artists of the city. Nevertheless, the creation business is not a nine-to-five job; it is all-consuming and living next to your work can be a great solution.

If you get into building codes, however, be prepared for a lot of conflicting 'official' opinions. I testified when Washington, D.C., held hearings on trying to copy other loft laws. The problem was, as I predicted, that although they passed the law allowing living as an accessory use in industrial buildings under certain conditions, they did not determine what building codes had to be followed. Should artists put electrical outlets in their living portions every twelve feet as demanded by residential codes, or can they maintain industrial building codes? More importantly, the new law never trickled down to the many field inspectors who, more than a dozen years after the measure passed, still had no idea about it nor any better idea of what an 'artist's studio' is. If you get caught in this bureaucratic trap, you'd better be patient and have a good lawyer.

In New York City, hundreds of buildings were targeted for the loft law that was passed in 1982. Presently, most of these buildings have not been brought up to loft code, due largely to the complications of following the new codes and the prohibited costs. Consequently, artists by the hundreds inhabit studios unlawfully, and then get thrown out en masse when the city finally gets wind of them.

Many artists have a permanent, legal address somewhere else and just work 'late' at night. A bed for 'napping,' a kitchenette for lunch, and a 'safety' shower are justified for an ordinary work environment.

The commute to the studio is an important consideration. Being next to your work, day and night, makes it easy for you to work. A demanding family can make concentration difficult. One time, I had the best of both worlds; my studio was two blocks from our house. I could walk home for dinner, and after the children were in bed, go back to work. When my studio later moved and it was a fifteen-minute drive across town, I had less energy to make the commute back in the evening, just to put in an hour or two of work. And imagine having an hour commute.

CHAPTER 2
Real-Estate Matters

The best deals are buildings that are structurally and mechanically sound, but look a mess.

Weeds growing in front of entrances are to artists in search of studio space what chocolate truffles are to other people.

HOW TO LOOK

Pick a region of the country, a state, an area, a city or town. There will be many elements governing this decision. Usually – and this is something to think about – artists do not say to themselves, "Where do I want to live and work?" Places are normally decided upon by job, family, or other obligations. Perhaps it is time to examine and see if these connections are still important or vital.

Even if there's an obligation to live in a specific area, a commute of an hour or less might be acceptable. In most cases, this would give you the option of urban, suburban or rural living.

Artists usually look for lower-income, economically distressed areas. Pick an area and drive around; this should become your recreational hobby until you have finally secured a permanent studio space. Spend at least one lunch hour a week, and every other Saturday spend a few hours looking around. Ask around. Most people who have distressed properties do not advertise their predicaments. You will be surprised how much information you can find out about a property simply by knocking on the building next door, the nearest business, or the nearest bank. Look around for deferred maintenance, which is a nice way of saying that people who have money problems can't keep up with exterior repairs.

The best deals are buildings that are structurally and mechanically sound, but look a mess. I am always amazed at how many properties are turned down by prospects just because of cosmetics. When we renovated the mill, we filled up forty huge dumpsters with debris, but underneath all the trash was a structurally and mechanically sound building.

Look around no matter where you are, especially when you travel. I needed a large-scale studio space to carry out ambitious projects. I knew I couldn't do it in the studio I then occupied, so I thought a second, summer studio that would not need to be heated, might work. In addition to thinking about finding more space near where I was already based, I considered (very casually) an unfinished structure on a Greek island during one vacation, a country barn during another driving trip, and later, an eastern Pennsylvania mill. Sometimes our weekend recreational drives were centered in an area where I wanted to look for property; other times, I included looking at real estate during our family outings. The mill I am working and living in now came about when I went to a new area to try a new process at a plastics R&D facility. I had never been to this area, and it was never my intention to move here.

I always had my 'dream studio' in mind, so I was always on the watch. You never know what is waiting around the curve, down the alley, or on the other side of the block. I look for old buildings the way beach combers look for shells.

Luckily for artists, the United States is a treasure trove. You will be in studio heaven in the United States compared to your colleagues in other countries, where studios are small cubicles and everything is expensive and creative building projects are difficult to carry out.

Study national trends, but also observe how these trends have trickled down to your area. While jobs have gone elsewhere, what has been left behind is a vast storage of empty manufacturing buildings. Similarly, populations have moved out of the cities to nearby suburbs, leaving downtowns to decay. Even many materials needed to fix up a studio (and to make art) can be readily found in dumpsters and scrap yards all over the place, as well as in the many "Going Out of Business - Fixtures Included" closing sales.

As the Wal-Marts and shopping centers are forcing traditional businesses to close, artists can pick up the crumbs.

Read the local newspapers. Articles will tell you what businesses are closing, what buildings are of a concern to neighbors, and who's in trouble. I found my way to my mill because I happened to pick up a free weekly newspaper and read about a mill the town wanted to tear down because no one could find use for it. My inquiry about that mill led me to the one I finally did purchase.

With the huge stock of property, there are always some bargains. Those are the ones artists can cash in on. By the way, at times I've been asked if buying at such low prices, or in a foreclosure sale (which I also have attended), is like becoming a vulture and feeding upon people and businesses that are down on their luck. The positive way of looking at it is that people might be desperate to sell but there is no market. For people needing to sell, some money might be better than no money, so I would not worry about making low offers for properties. Sometimes only artists can justify purchasing a white elephant.

This industrial building is begging for new ownership!

Go over the following list before you drive around. It may stimulate you to consider buildings that you would otherwise drive by without noticing. Obviously, you want to look for businesses that have closed or look as if they might close any day. Weeds growing in front of entrances are to artists in search of studio space what chocolate truffles are to other people.

Gas stations	Bowling alleys
Dry cleaners	Movie theaters
Retail stores	Barns
Garages	Motels
Churches	Office buildings
5 & 10 stores	Schools
Restaurants	Night clubs
Banks	Grocery stores
Drugstores	Lumberyards
Apartment buildings	Houses
Strip shopping centers	Factories
Libraries	Corner stores
Stables	Bakeries
Car repair shops	Car dealers
Hotels	Warehouses
City-owned properties	Military buildings

Talk to people, wherever you are, about your need for a studio. My wife was a dental hygienist and she didn't want me to buy a (great) studio I found in Baltimore, since we were in Washington; she knew the long commute would not be good for the family. While having the ears of whomever she was working on, she would mention our plight. One patient was a real-estate agent who just happened to know about the situation that allowed me to buy the 34,000-square-foot warehouse much closer to home. Many other prospective studios were also discovered initially by conversation. Talk to business people who are also interested in the arts. They might not even be thinking about real estate, but know of a business about to fold, and "now that you think about it, there would be an empty warehouse resulting." This is the kind of information you get only by being vocal and active.

LOCATION, LOCATION, LOCATION

In real estate, there's the saying that the important elements are location, location and location. It's the same for art studios. Location will determine if it's affordable space. There is no sense looking in the equivalent of Beverly Hills, Georgetown, SoHo (now), or Miami Beach, unless you have lots of money.

Neighborhoods. Where should you look? What regions of the country, then what cities, then what neighborhoods? Do you need intellectual art support? Do you need artists nearby? Do you need access to galleries, museums, critics, collectors or other culture? Can you teach or be employed? Is the area safe or not, and can you deal with that? Will your spouse, friends or family be affected by the location? Can you even go down the street for lunch?

Access to Supplies. Are you not only mentally able to work alone, if necessary, but can you also work without easily getting supplies, technical assistance and other resources? FedEx and UPS will go practically anywhere, but often you still need to drive for large supplies and services. I live in a small city (although it is rich in culture), and it's much faster for me to do errands than when I lived in a large city. But if I lived in a more rural town, I wouldn't have the lumberyard, plumbing-supply and hardware stores within a few minutes of my studio.

Specialized Processes and Facilities. Most artists change their styles and mediums, but at the same time, they know their basic needs. If you weld sculptures, you might want access to a facility that has raw materials or a computer-controlled plasma cutter, for example. I wanted access to industrial polycarbonate blow-molding equipment. I also needed help repairing my polyurethane foam equipment and incorporating robotic systems into my sculptures. Some of it may not be 'up the street,' but being in one state may make life a whole lot easier than being in another state.

Practicalities. Practical matters count. Most artists need to be employed, whether that means teaching or driving a taxi. Look around a potential studio region and carefully note job opportunities. For practical aspects of life, check if there are convenient grocery stores and drugstores nearby. What about car repairs – if you have little money, you probably have an older car, and if it breaks down, are there repair places nearby? What about the doctor and the hospital? How far away is the post office? Some of these places are usually visited several times a week, and if takes an hour by car to get there, that represents a lot of wasted time.

If you are looking in a large city and you have a family, will you be able to go out, find baby sitters, enroll your children in good schools, or even just play or walk outside? These might seem like very uninteresting issues, but time is of importance.

Cost of Living. There is a world of difference between having a studio in New York City and having a studio in North Adams, (western) Massachusetts, located to the north three hours by car. I will make an argument that, depending on where your career is, there are better opportunities away from New York. But both are income-driven. If you are earning $150,000 a year, then the big city may be fine. If you can afford the rental of a decent-sized loft in a good neighborhood, then that situation may work for you, especially if you are painting moderate-sized works and they are moving out the door steadily enough to minimize storage. However, if you need more space, then you run into problems in the city.

For a fraction of NYC costs, you can have everything you need in a smaller community, where the cost of living for almost everything is lower. But there is a catch. You won't have the access to the same income unless you can do work via the Internet. This rule used to be true in most metropolitan areas. As you drifted away from the city's nucleus, real estate got cheaper, mostly because an absence of land suitable for building drove up the values. This was the main thrust for developing the suburbs. Now, however, the suburbs have become metropolitan centers, and in many cities the inner core neighborhoods have suffered.

Neighborhood Potential. When you look for a studio location, you must not only look for the current state of affairs, but where the neighborhood is going and how close it is to present growth areas. If the area is improving, your property will appreciate; whether you sell it someday or borrow against it, it will still allow more options in the future. If the neighborhood is being discovered, a la NYC's SoHo in the 1960s, then you have additional options. Will your studio also be a base for selling? Will collectors come? Artists always think that they are in some forgotten ghetto working away, but a decade later the area has become a hot spot, and the buildings then can provide settings for galleries, eateries, performance spaces and a host of commerce opportunities.

A Lost Opportunity: A Case Study. Artists as a group, to be blunt, are bad in business and slow at getting through the door. In Washington, D.C., I tried with other artists to take over a complex that would have made a major impact on the art scene, but eventually I simply did my own thing, and artists who participated did so only as renters. In North Adams, Massachusetts, site of a major contemporary art museum drawing an international audience, and near the world renowned Clark Art Institute, the Williams College Museum of Art, and an art conservation center as well as our Contemporary Artists Center (just to name players in the visual arts), there was a wonderful opportunity. A mill of 110,000 square feet just a few blocks from MASS MoCA was for sale. For six years, I tried to talk artists into jointly buying the mill. The idea was that they could have second studios if not main studios, and the rental of some of the space would mean that, in just a few years, the original artists would not only have free studio space, but income as well. Exhibition and performance space could also have been part of the package. Not only was this mill cheap per square foot, as was mentioned earlier, but it is also an important example because the opportunity lost was really more than about cheap workspace. It could have provided artists with a chance to show and participate in an area that clearly was about to explode. Today, artists are clamoring for this type of space, but it's a bit late to participate in this particular deal.

It is not always obvious which areas will boom, but neither is it always hidden. With a little practice looking for the signs, you can usually see when a neighborhood has 'bottomed out' price-wise, just like a stock, and when outside forces will stimulate a rapid recovery.

If you think I might be some real-estate genius and others can't do it, I'm not. My track record is based on what I regard as 'no-brainers.' It's simply that few other artists have bothered to look for the possibilities.

What to Eyeball. As you read the rest of this manual, you will learn about various aspects of construction, mechanical and structural systems, hazardous wastes, and other aspects you will need to study if you are considering an old, industrial property. Once you have selected a prospective property, you will read about specific steps to take. But in the early stages, when you are just driving around, asking people you meet and mostly seeing buildings from the outside, or at best during a quick inside tour, you need to know a few things to look for in order to determine if the property is worth further consideration.

I've looked at many buildings that were just shells, without any mechanical systems at all. In this case, you want to know about the roof, about whether water and sewer are connected to the building, and what it would take to get electricity to the property, as well as gas or oil for heat. Most of your renovation calculations will be for new work.

Usually you can tell what is going on just from the outside. You can look for old signs indicating what type of business used to operate there. You can peek through windows and see if there are any indications of recent use. You can look for dumpsters, old trucks, and loading-dock items to get clues about how recently the property was in use. You can look for weeds, growing not only on the ground, but also on the roof and in gutters. You can look for broken windows, a sure sign that the property has been left alone for quite some time.

The majority of the properties you will look at will probably have a history of use. The more recent the better.

Hopefully, there will be working systems for heat, electricity and plumbing. Art studios seldom need more electrical power than a building will already have. If the heating system works to some degree, you can always beef it up in some critical areas. And if there is one bathroom, you are all set. If there are more, you can easily think about subdividing the space if there is ample room.

Electrical, plumbing and heating work is expensive. If you can avoid doing a lot of repairs in these areas, so much the better. Don't worry about the toilet fixtures; look at the pipes. Look to see if lights work, if outlets have three holes for grounding, and if the panel boxes have circuit breakers (switches) rather than the old-style fuses.

Interior walls are easy to build. That is never a concern if you have lots of space to play with. They can be repaired quickly as well. The cost is so great for new electrical service to a property that it is much more of a concern than superficial wall damage.

Later, I've provided a checklist of all the components you will need to keep in mind as you look for properties, but on the first go-around, these are the basic ones.

'Novel' Gets Old. Before you get too excited about a space, pay attention to some of the pitfalls. I've known hundreds of artists who have had all kinds of weird situations. Almost always, these odd types of situations are laughed about or seem cute at the time. Like having to climb out a window to get into the work area. Or having to take the wastewater from a temporary holding tank down a hallway and into a proper drain. But after a while these things become a source of annoyance. And I also know that when winter comes, or when the artist has to move equipment in or out, these oddities can become real detriments for getting good use out of a space.

Sometimes the landlord will look the other way about artists living in the studio, and conversely, the artists will be grateful for the low rent. The most common problem are buildings, which artists have gotten cheaply as rentals, which are inadequately heated. A bargain space that artists expect to use for twelve months of the year becomes less of a bargain if it is usable for only seven months.

Make Your Studio Free. In the mix of possibilities, money is usually the overriding concern and limitation. You can purchase a studio building and make it cheaper than renting, but to get the discount per square foot, you need to buy a lot. If you rent out portions of your space, you can even arrange it so that the rented portion pays for all of your expenses. There are people who simply choose to rent and will rent from you if you supply the individual spaces.

If you go this route, renting out to others instead of renting yourself, you may feel that it will become a full-time job. It might during the construction period, but after the building is rented, it will take between five and ten hours per week. But your time will be compensated, because you can end up with a gigantic studio for your own use at no additional expense. Also, when the debt has been paid down, you will receive income in addition to the free space. Owning a valuable asset someday, you will have even more opportunities to help your art.

This manual will still be pertinent for artists and creators who must rent. However, one day a building will appear and you will want to grab it on a permanent basis. Purchasing old buildings need not take as much cash or expense as you first might think.

RENT OR MORTGAGE?

Leasing. The emphasis of this book is to concentrate on purchasing space so that artists will lock into permanent space and be in complete control. There are circumstances, however, where leasing is a viable alternative.

Don't Lease. I will mention group artists' buildings often; they can be established in a variety of ways. I've found that the most common way is when an ambitious artist finds big space, is unable to purchase it, and enters into a 'cheap' rental agreement with the owner. He or she then attracts artist friends and the building fills up with economic space. This is all fine as long as it lasts. The problem is that it won't last for more than a few years.

That would be also fine if new space would be easy

to find. Most often, it gets more and more difficult to find studio space, and the rents keep going up. The other tragic aspect of this scenario is that the artists are going through all the work and most of the risk of taking on large space. So why not purchase it instead? Usually the excuse is financial; in my estimation, a bit more knowledge about real estate will change the artist's view.

If you are intent on leasing a large space because of some unusual opportunity, then all the planning, construction and operational aspects of this book are especially valid. My only opinion is that you should purchase, instead of rent, but I'm sure that some of you will still jump into rental 'deals' that are too good to pass up.

This 24,000 square-foot building had a good run; artists took over the raw space and divided it into twenty studios. They pushed the landlord to make at least a few improvements, such as patching the roof. It was economic and lasted twenty years. The owner now wants to cash in and will be evicting the artists within a year or so. If they had bought the space in the beginning, it would still be going strong.

Finding a Rental Studio. Most artists rent studios. It's the simplest way to get working requiring the least amount of time and money. But even finding a good rental studio can be tough.

If you look at city versus rural, east or west coast versus interior states, you will immediately see some differences. For a rough comparison, and depending on neighborhood, of course, $1,000 per month will get you about 700 square feet in New York and San Francisco. It will get you more than 1,000 square feet in Chicago and Los Angeles. It will get you 1,500 square feet in Washington, D.C. It will get you 4,000 square feet in North Adams (western), Massachusetts, and probably in any small town in the United States (especially in areas where a Porsche or Mercedes is rarely seen).

Within the rental market, there are deals. In Washington, D.C., when artists were renting second-floor walkups in narrow commercial row houses, I found gigantic ground-floor space for less rent than others were paying for a fifth of the space. In my searches I found several great studios to choose from, while other artists were having trouble finding any suitable studio space. Why? I looked where space was being overlooked. In the case of Washington, before the condominium craze, the city was filled with big, old apartment buildings. Many of these buildings had full basements for storage, and some of these had windows. Not all the space was in use. While most artists were looking up at second- and third-floor windows, I was walking down into the basements of every large building I could find. Of course, after condominium conversions became the hot item, all space in apartment buildings became scrutinized and valuable.

Everything that is discussed in finding studio space to purchase can also be applied for rental space.

There is a tremendous discount for renting quantity. If you want a small, individual studio, it will cost you a lot more per square foot than if you organize a few colleagues and rent a large space to accommodate all of you. This is a key to getting better space.

I used to say that even if I rented a closet to someone, I would have to charge $250 per month in rent. Why? Because there is an expense in someone just walking in the door to work, using bathrooms, utilities, doors, loading docks, elevators and public floor areas, creating more wear and tear, possible breakage, and an equal share of some utilities. Renting a larger space does not demand more maintenance by the landlord, especially if the tenant is paying for the heat and electricity. A larger studio will probably still have one heater, although a bit larger, and perhaps a few more windows, but windows are low-maintenance.

Generally speaking, from a landlord's perspective, one tenant taking a lot of space is much preferable to several smaller ones, with two exceptions. First, there is more risk that one tenant will leave, and therefore the landlord will lose income until the space can be rented again; if one smaller tenant leaves, the landlord still has income from the other tenants. Second, a landlord can usually bump up the square- foot rate considerably for the smaller studios, in order to offset the additional maintenance expenses and to achieve greater profits. So if the rental market for smaller studios is strong, landlord/developers will probably opt to spend more on the fix-up to partition the spaces in order to capitalize on the rental rates. That is, if the landlord is also a developer. Most are not. So artist/developers can profit if they can realize their markets; artists are usually very aware of their colleagues' needs and know the market better than the owners.

But the second part of this is that if you are the one to find the space and to gather together the participants, shouldn't you be rewarded for your efforts by getting extra space for free? This is how many real-estate developers operate.

Square-Foot Rentals. Rental rates for commercial and industrial space vary depending on location. For example, in major cities office space may rent for $50 to $100 per square foot. In small towns away from metropolitan areas, decent office space may rent for $5 to $10 per square foot. Industrial space may rent for only $5 per square foot, because this type of space is often found in the outskirts of town, where land is cheaper and one-story construction is possible. It may require, however, renting thousands of feet at a time.

In case you do not know how to calculate costs when you are given a square-foot rental rate, the following may help. If there is a space of 1,000 square feet and someone is asking $10 per square foot, that means that it is $10 multiplied by the 1,000 square feet, which gives the annual cost of $10,000 in this example. The $10,000 is divided by twelve months, giving you a monthly rental of $833.33. Of course, utilities, maintenance, and other costs may also be added to this. In addition, the rate is calculated according to the size of the space that is presented. The actual size of the space may be greater or smaller than the footage you have agreed to pay on, depending on how the landlord does his figuring. The landlord may be adding square footage to cover for the thickness of exterior walls or public hallway areas. In some areas, San Francisco for example, the asking rental is given in monthly numbers. So instead of asking $10 per square foot, a landlord may ask $.83 per square foot, which means per month and is the same as $10 per square foot per year. It only gets confusing when you come from a small town where $.83 could mean per year.

If you live in a metropolitan area, you can easily check rentals in the classified ads. You will get a feeling for the value of space. Generally speaking, no matter where in the country you live, artists have limited income. In many cases, the monthly amount an artist can afford will not vary significantly, just the size of the space that a specific amount can rent. If you have followed rentals for a while, you will also know that they have gone up considerably over the past ten years. They might come down for a while, as businesses close, but if the economy picks up, then there will be pressure again to increase rates.

While many buildings could offer reasonable rent at $5 to $15 per square foot, my advice is to think in terms of less than $2 per square foot. Less than $1 is even more attractive. You might not find even raw land for that low price, let alone a studio space with a roof, heat, electricity and water. Obviously, you need to make adjustments as to whether you plan on working in New York or Kansas, but no matter where, there will remain a large discrepancy between what artists can afford and the going rate. However, this book aims at narrowing this gap.

Sharing the space. Take a four-thousand-foot studio space, for example. At a reasonable $5 per square foot rental (certainly not in most urban centers), it would cost $20,000 a year, or a monthly rental of $1,666. This might be too much for one artist to pay for a separate working space. Most artists would then turn to much smaller spaces.

If you could divide the studio into fourths, and rent out two quarter-units for $600 each, the remaining two quarters (2,000 square feet) would cost you $466 per month. This would give you a square-foot rental of $2.80, which gets closer to my goal of having a less than $2 rental (and this deals with rentals only; purchasers will find much better options). I mention renting out the other half of the space as two quarter-units because it may be easier to find two artists who can afford $600 each than one artist who can afford $1,200.

At the very least, share a space with one other artist. For example, if $1,000 rents a 1,500-square-foot studio, $500 probably rents you just 500 square feet. If you share the 1,500-square-foot space with someone (you can easily build an eight-foot partition which will give you more privacy as well as additional wall area), each of you will get extra space for free because your $500 will bring you 750 square feet.

The developer should get some financial reward. As will be discussed at length, if you are finding the space and getting either income or better space for your efforts, why not do the same thing, but by purchasing the space rather than renting it? This way, you can enjoy either free space or income. This income can increase each year, rather than your rent.

First Studios. There are reasons to rent. Artists or creators just starting their careers will have little money and may not even know what type of work they will carry out or where they will locate. Many artists take teaching jobs, and that will dictate their destinations. Additionally, they may move into a studio knowing full well that they won't be there in two years, and that might be acceptable. Artists will put in as much time in organizing and fixing up a space as the length of use determines. If you are only going to be there two years, you might spend a week and a few hundred dollars for materials to bring the studio up to your standards, but you certainly won't spend thousands of dollars and months of time to do the same. After all, your time may not be worth much, but it's worth something. Your time for making art is short and much more important.

This is the way many young artists get started, and there is nothing wrong with it. Knowing what to look for in a potential new studio is important, however. I've known many artists who rent a space thinking it will only take a few days to get into order, only to move in and find out that there are severe problems which have to be fixed before they can work. Studying the construction and renovation sections of this book will help you, whether the space is being rented or purchased. Reading about commercial leases will help you avoid disasters.

Artists also rent studios because they must, but they are keeping their eyes open for a better situation. This is the type of creator who will benefit the most from reading this book. Gold mines are abundant, but they are not found in a day or two.

This studio is not large, only 350 square feet, but at $275 per month, including utilities, in Washington, D.C., it's a bargain and a perfect 'first studio' or for small works. (Jeweler Emma Villedrouin)

No Choice. Artists who decide to be in New York City, for example, do so for access to the art scene. Certainly, early in a career, there is nothing quite like the Big Apple. It is also a humbling place, where a visual artist might be competing for gallery shows with several hundred thousands of other artists. It puts a lot in perspective. Life consists of tradeoffs. If the city is the place to be, then the search is for the best studio that a limited budget can rent in a neighborhood that is the least dangerous and least remote from the action.

No Time. Artists need time to work, and some periods are busier than others. This year may not be the time to spend on real estate when shows are scheduled and work has to get done. Certainly, renting a studio where little has to be done other than to move in has huge advantages when one is under the gun. Let the landlord worry about leaks, insurance, and building codes.

Keep in mind, however, that the flip side of this argument is being under the same pressures, and being forced out when the owner decides to raise the rent or change the character of the property.

Special Deals. Artists rent because there are special deals. I had one of the biggest studios in Washington, D.C., when I found an apartment-building owner with a vacant street-level floor space. A restaurant had once operated there and had a fire. When I came upon it, the space had dirt-filled trenches where pipes had been repaired, and piles of trash. It wasn't going to be rented to any commercial tenant without one or both parties doing a major renovation, requiring a substantial investment. For rent that barely covered the heat and electric bill, I had 6,000 square feet, just blocks from the galleries and four blocks from our house. It was a deal too good to turn down at the time. I wasn't going to buy a place when I had one of the deals of a lifetime. (Besides, I didn't have access to The Art Studio/Loft Manual back then!)

Artists sometimes find spaces connected to companies where their work is carried out. One sculptor had a studio adjacent to a quarry in space that was underutilized; a metal sculptor found a studio in the back of a welding shop. The value is not just the empty space, but also the access to other equipment.

If you are lucky, you can cultivate real-estate owners who also happen to be collectors. Fast money in real estate goes hand in hand with art galleries and the art scene. Many property owners have oddball spaces that do not fit traditional rentals. Perhaps one of these business people can be generous to you and make you an offer of space in exchange for art. Who would turn that down? Just make sure a bargain deal is indeed a bargain. Something that lasts only about a year and involves a lot of up-front work by you is not a great deal. A twenty-year lease may be.

Lease Contracts. Be careful what you sign; read, read and read again the boring small print. Basically, you need to know how much per month you will pay, how long you are obligated to pay (the term), and who pays for electricity, heat and hot water, taxes, telephone, water and sewer, and maintenance.

You also need to know if what you sign could become your worst nightmare. Does the lease allow any "new expenses" to be charged to you?

Normally, if there are individual electric or gas meters, the tenant pays for those utilities. The landlord usually pays for water because it can't be individually metered for each space. If you are renting just one space and there are several others in the building, normally your rent will be what you pay, plus perhaps a maintenance fee that is locked in.

If, on the other hand, you are renting an entire building, you may be asked to pay "triple net," which means that you pay for everything, including taxes, all maintenance, utilities and insurance – in addition to your rent. (You might as well own at that point.) Often, landlords may ask for annual rent increases, sometimes based on the Consumer Price Index, which is a governmental index that tells you how much the cost of living is going up (inflation). A common plan just locks in 3% to 5% increases each year.

Another main thing to worry about is what happens after your term is up. If you have paid, for example, $600 per month for two years, will your rent be increased to $1,200 per month? This uncertainty has worried many artists, and unfortunately there is cause for this concern. As was stated, the activity of art can improve neighborhoods, and after artists have done the hard part, their rents are jacked up.

Always keep in mind that if you find a cheap rental studio, it is cheap because the owner cannot find someone to pay more. When the market improves, the owner will want more, regardless of the fact that you are a nice person and have fixed up the space on your own. If you don't have a written deal spelling out the length and the increases, you will not be there when someone else is willing to rent the space for more.

My Washington warehouse turned studio/loft building has twenty-five studios and has been going strong since 1978. I often cringe when I watch an artist sign a lease without even reading it. They happen to be safe with me, but I could, though I won't, write another book filled with horror stories.

Mostly, you want to keep the space if the rent is low. Sometimes you want to move on. Unfortunately, many artists with few liquid assets think they can break a lease and leave whenever they want, especially after not paying rent for two or three months. The truth is, they often can get away with it because the cost of going after them makes it impractical, especially since, even if there is a judgment from the court, the landlord probably can't collect if the artist has no money.

The flip side is that these are the artists who are not going to get long-term satisfactory studio space. They won't have the good references to rent or buy outstanding studios. I've helped many, many artists over the years, and I can tell you that rarely do these types of artists surface and become successful. I really don't care because I'm not here to preach, but if you are interested in doing ambitious work in gigantic work quarters, don't cut off your tail to spite yourself. Play fair with others and good fortune will smile on you. When you find your deal of a lifetime, you won't have a history of negative issues to interfere with it.

Ignorance. This is the main reason artists rent. In almost all cases where an artist is renting, for the same amount of money he/she could own a bigger space. In most of these same cases, rents will go up each year, and within five years the artist will have to find new quarters.

Many artists are doing just fine, income-wise. They are teaching, their spouses work, they are selling, or they have some family support. These are the artists who are purchasing medium-sized studio/condos for $150,000 or more (in many city markets). The spaces usually vary from 700 square feet to 1,800 square feet. These are the artists who are most likely to spend $1,000 or more per month for their studio space, and more importantly, they are spending an equal amount for peripheral activities – slides taken by others, fancy resumes and business cards, yellow-page listings, store-bought drafting tables, web sites, and so forth. These artists might even be paying for

Part of a medium-sized photography studio; notice the partial walls that still allow heat to reach adjacent studios; exposed beams and wood floors give it a nice feeling; from a sculptor's point of view, photographers have it made, space-wise.

separate apartments or houses. These are the artists who are paying retail; they could be paying wholesale or less.

I would suggest that concentrating on two areas, studio space and direct art expense, is a much better way to organize resources.

PURCHASING

Why rent when you can own? This is an advertising slogan used everywhere, but it is relevant to artists. You pay dearly for the convenience of having others worry about your studio space. If the art business were such a financially rewarding enterprise, this book wouldn't be necessary and rentals would be acceptable. But when you have few resources, it is important that they be used wisely. And while there is definitely an extra amount of effort needed in the beginning to deal with a property, it will pay off royally as you continue to make art.

Another idea that needs to stay with you while you get into the details is that you don't necessarily need a lot of money to purchase. I have always had a positive cash flow in my real-estate projects, and if you can put in the extra work in the beginning (some of which you have to, whether you rent or not) you can make a free studio happen.

Purchase. Purchasing studio space is certainly cheaper in the long run. As you picture this mentally, I don't necessarily mean purchasing just one studio by itself. I mean purchasing a monster of a space, which could be a studio just for you, or it could be a space with room for others.

Improvements may be made over a longer period of time, and may be enjoyed over the life of the occupancy. Obviously, like a house, the building might go up in value. Artists can benefit from this down the road by borrowing against the appreciated value, selling the property in order to move into something better, or simply enjoy having a studio that is worth more. If the location were questionable at the time of purchase, it is very likely that after a few years of 'arts use,' the surrounding environment will be a much better place. Certainly, it is a great feeling to have a studio space with the debt locked in or even paid off, and to know what it would cost if rented or bought today.

Purchasing space gives the artist many more options - how to use it, or whether to divide it into different parts. Dividing and renting out space also gives you the option to expand into that space in the future. It also assures that improvements stay with you. You are not improving someone else's property, but your own.

How you use the property in five years may, and the odds are it will, be different from how you use the property in the first few months. In our case, it was never our first intention, but we decided with excess space to start an artists' studio organization, and ended up including five exhibition spaces with a full schedule of shows and events. In another example, I searched for large, additional studio space to build a prototype installation/exhibition that was on my active list for fifteen years. When I found the mill, I had space to carry out the project. However, my intention was for the project to be exhibited in a traditional museum. When no museum would take it, even with a big-name curator supporting it, and when first-floor space in the mill became available, I constructed it there. When I moved here, I never thought the public testing ground for the exhibition would be in my own studio building. Having extra space provided me that option; it remains on view longer than a museum would ever have scheduled it. As a work in progress I can develop it over the years.

The bigger the property, the more choices are out there. Many small firms, employing fewer than a dozen people, look for industrial properties to fit their needs. Most are looking for 2,000 to 5,000 square feet. Owners of large warehouses of 50,000 square feet, for example, have trouble finding purchasers, because any company needing that much space probably also needs a one-story space in a modern facility. At the same time, owners seldom have the wherewithal to develop and partition large spaces themselves. Nor do they know the 'art market.' So buildings sit. These are the properties to look at. If others are after them, then you won't get a good deal; if no one wants it, it might have potential for an art purpose.

This is a key point that I feel compelled to emphasize. If the market for traditional rentals is weak in an area, but there is an abundance of artists in the area, only an artist knows best how to tap that potential market. Using this knowledge will enable you to make sense of a property purchase where others cannot.

A Case Study. In 1978, I was forced to move out of my large, 6,000-square-foot studio where I had been paying such low rent that it probably didn't even cover my utilities. Finally I found an old, four-story brick warehouse that had been vacant for eight years. Although it was not in a great neighborhood, houses being renovated on the same street were being sold for $72,000. The entire 34,000-square-foot building was only $66,000, and the owners gave me a mortgage of $60,000. I then borrowed a few thousand dollars and renovated the basement into six small studios. With confidence (and income) from that success, I went back to the bank. I soon took out another bank loan to partition and renovate the building into basic studio/lofts. Within a couple of years, I was renting fifteen studios in the building, plus one large 'second' gallery for my dealer at the time, who needed cheap additional loft space to show large sculptures. I had positive cash flow the entire time.

Best of all, I had a gigantic studio for my own use. I would like to say for free, which it was, but, admittedly, I 'paid' by being janitor, leasing agent, owner, contractor, and all-around trouble-shooter. Within two years, two adjacent buildings had filled up with artists. Years later, I partitioned my huge studio into five large studios, and this income paid for the bulk of my move to an even larger facility.

Today, the building has twenty-five studios (after I moved to larger quarters) and the building is worth fifteen times the purchase price. There have been few vacancies over the years, and the small turnover of studios is quickly filled. You can see that it worked for me in several ways: by giving me immediate space at no cost, by allowing expansion, by financing a move to a larger studio complex, and by becoming an asset. Also important were the activities and interactions with artists and visitors. The building became an important nerve center for creative work.

I was ready to buy this even without seeing the inside; I knew the square footage (34,000), the price ($66,000) and the location. A closer inspection showed more positive elements, and it came with owner financing.

Timing. As I just mentioned, when deals are passed up, it is too late a year later to resurrect them. You might also get an impression that you are ten years too late. When I talk about getting a property for $66,000, which today is worth many times that, you will wonder where the deals are today. Of course, many neighborhoods that were bargains two decades ago are now out of the question. But this doesn't mean that now isn't a good time to buy property.

When we used to look for property in the country (I was exploring the possibility of studios in barns), everyone used to say, " You should have been here five years ago." But five years later, the same thing was being said.

In my present community, I can say that five years

ago there were incredible deals, and it is a pity that artists didn't see them. At the same time, as I write this, I know a few buildings that could still be incredible deals, and five years from now some artists will be kicking themselves for not getting them. In fact, currently one artist/entrepreneur is going after one of the last small mills available in the area: 15,000 square feet for about $50,000. If he can rent out two floors, it will pay for the purchase and fix-up costs, while giving him 6,000 square feet for free. The building is about four blocks away from MASS MoCA, an international contemporary art museum. Another property of 80,000 square feet may be available for $130,000 - ample space to make it work economically. There is a duplex (two houses together) for sale less than two blocks from the museum. The asking price is just $24,000. It has commercial potential. Get to know your area, because there is more than one deal in town.

The point is that there are always opportunities, but of course, the earlier you get in, the better.

NEGOTIATION

It's a game; there are no two ways of saying it. Artists must get 'streetwise.' It's no different. If you have ever been to markets in third-world countries, you'll know what I'm talking about. Try shopping on Orchard Street the next Sunday you are in New York City; or go shopping for a car. It's a cat-and-mouse game, and you will need to practice.

Cash on Hand. Yep, it takes money to buy real estate. But the seller doesn't need to know your financial shortcomings. Pretend you come from a good family with lots of cash. Always look for property as if you could simply write out a check if you wanted to. The idea is not to look as though you are in need - let the seller be the one in need.

I've watched artists stumble upon some good potential studio buildings, and then stumble completely in talking to the owner or agent; they sound as if they could barely buy a ten-year-old car, let alone a large property. I've never known one of them to be successful. The artists

I've observed who come across convincingly, however, have been successful in their acquisitions. (I am not alone in this endeavor.)

If you seem like you can't conclude the deal, the seller will want more money up front to see if you are for real. If you seem like you have the cash to do the deal, and if the seller is somewhat anxious to sell (but won't show that, of course), you will have a better chance of getting the property on your terms.

What are your terms? You want the property for the lowest price possible and with as little cash down as possible. More realistically, the goal is to lock in an option on the property (i.e., to get it under a signed sales agreement) so that you have time to shop it around and find some financing, investors, partners, tenants, or backers before you have to actually pay a deposit which would be lost if you didn't go through with the purchase.

Keep in mind that the more you know about the building the better you can negotiate. You have, hopefully, checked with neighbors to learn about problems. You can go down to the city or county records office and find out the last purchase price, the appraised value (which will determine the real-estate taxes) and if the owner has a mortgage. The records won't show the balance of the mortgage but will show the originating date, and you can estimate easily whether or not a lot of money is owed to the bank. You can also determine whether a low offer will be accepted. If the owner owes the bank, he/she probably will not accept an offer of less than the amount that has to be paid back to the bank. You might even find out that back taxes are owed, a sure sign that the owner needs to sell.

I knew a professional real-estate investor whose average offers were about one half of the offered price. Now if a house, for example, is for sale at $100,000, it is a bit embarrassing to offer $50,000. You know it's way out of line – right? Well, this investor's philosophy was that you only get one out of fifty, but that one is really a deal! He wasn't afraid of being told to get lost. In other words, don't be shy. Some properties might not be worth even 50% of the asking price. And it doesn't take long to make fifty offers, because until someone bites, it's only a piece of paper. Only the property address and dollar offer changes on the contract being offered. Some investors make offers for buildings costing megabucks the way you and I might buy tires.

Who says what first? Never make an offer out of the blue. You need to know more facts. The best way is to get a number from the seller. You might be surprised how low the asking price is. Then you can get him/her down from there. Owners of old properties that are in neglect rarely have a sense of their potential. If they were developers or entrepreneurs or knew about the arts, they would have developed the properties themselves.

Never seem anxious. It should almost seem that it's a bother to take it on because the renovation will probably cost more than it's worth. If you can't make this impression, just be quiet. All you really want to know is if the property is for sale and how much the owner is asking.

Never spend too much time on any property unless you get a firm price from the seller. Then try to concentrate only on getting a low price signed with a free out (as will be discussed), before you spend time on all the issues. Too many people get worked up about a property, thinking the owner will sell, when the owner is just using them to get a lot of information about the property's potential. Not only are they raising the owner's sense of what the property might be worth, they then might find out that the owner never really wanted to sell it. Not all old properties are for sale. There might be personal and family reasons, or just illusions about the property that don't fit reality. From my experience, don't fight an owner's logic; move on to another property.

Purchase Contract. Never, never, never accept a verbal deal. Many times I've seen an entrepreneur make a verbal understanding with an owner, then invite others to participate, or in other ways let it be known, and before anything has been signed, someone else comes along and takes the property by offering a bit more or better terms. In order to go from a verbal deal to one that is legally binding, a sales contract has to be signed by both parties. You don't need a real-estate agent involved to fill out a purchase agreement. You can get one online or go to a law supply store and pick up a boilerplate form. You can get one from a commercial real estate office if you know someone who will give you one. You can also just write up your offer. It need not be too complicated.

Purchase agreements have the following basic information included: Seller and purchaser names, address of the property, a simply description or a legal description so one can identify the property (i.e., 20,000 +/- square feet, building located on 1/4 acre, also known as 123 Studio Street), the total purchase price, the amount of deposit and when that deposit becomes not returnable to you (see next box), the settlement date, whether seller is taking back any financing, who pays for closing costs, and if any items are not included in the purchase. Also, there are clauses about what agents get. This is important if you sell a building, but not as important if you buy one and the seller pays the broker.

Standard 'boiler plate' purchase and sale agreements for commercial properties will contain many additional details, including: terms relating to adjustments (the seller pays all expenses up to settlement and the purchaser refunds to the seller money that the seller paid for taxes and services after settlement); title (the seller states he/she owns the property and has a right to sell it, and the seller has paid all taxes and liens up to or upon settlement); extensions (circumstances that would cause the agreed upon settlement date to be postponed); survey (sometimes one party or the other needs a survey of the property boundaries and agrees to pay for it); fixtures (often specific items attached to the property do not convey to the purchaser); hazardous wastes (states have differing laws pertaining to lead paint, asbestos, underground tanks and other potential hazardous wastes and what the seller must make known to the purchaser); condition of the property and utility services (depending on state law, various disclosures have to be made to the purchaser because the purchaser usually takes possession of the property "as is"); risk of loss (what happens if the property gets damaged after the agreement is signed but before settlement); disputes (what happens if there is a disagreement), and perhaps other details.

The essential items are what you should concentrate on initially. For example: Mr. ARTIST, (purchaser) in the name of an entity to be formed, agrees to buy from Ms. SELLER a property at 123 Studio Street, City, State, including a 20,000- square-foot (+/-) warehouse building with a six-bay garage on a quarter-acre lot, also known as Lot 123, Page 345, Book 67.

The purchase price will be $30,000 cash. A deposit of $3,000 has been paid, under the terms below. Upon settlement, the balance of $27,000 shall be paid in full. Settlement will be within 90 days of the date of this agreement, at a location of purchaser's choice.

Purchaser has 20 days from the date of this agreement to inspect the property. At the end of the inspection period, with written notice to seller, purchaser has the option to terminate this agreement, at purchaser's sole discretion, and all deposits shall be returned to purchaser. If no termination notice is given, then deposit shall become the property of the seller, and settlement shall be carried out according to the agreement. If purchaser defaults in the performance of this agreement, seller may retain the deposit as liquidated damages and both parties shall be released from all obligations under this agreement.

Seller and purchaser shall share 50-50 the expense of all transfer taxes and recordation fees. Taxes and utilities up to the settlement date shall be the responsibility of the seller. There are no agents or brokers involved with the sale.

Seller: to sign with date.
Purchaser: to sign with date.

This is not a well-written legal agreement; I just wanted to show you how simple it could be. The important clauses deal with having a free look without losing the deposit, and if you can, losing only the deposit (which you want to be as small as possible) if you fail to go through with the purchase. It is possible, although remote, that an owner can sue a prospective purchaser who does not complete the sale, especially if the owner has turned down other deals or is otherwise financially injured.

Also note that the purchaser named is you "in the name of an entity to be formed" because you haven't decided whose name or what kind of legal ownership there will be at settlement. Most likely you will want to form a separate company for the purchase. Speculators also do this to enable them to 'flip' the property for a quick profit.

Most likely, the above example could be enforced legally. I've purchased buildings with much less written, as represented below.

Example:

1. ARTIST, in the name of entity to be formed, to buy 123 Studio St. from SELLER COMPANY.
2. ARTIST to pay $30,000 cash, on or before April 1, 2002.
3. ARTIST has two weeks from date of signing to inspect property.
4. After two weeks, ARTIST will pay $2,000 as non-returnable deposit.
5. The Balance of $28,000 to be paid at settlement.
6. Property in "as is" condition, except that SELLER COMPANY shall clear debris.
7. Transfer and recordation fees shall be paid 50-50 by both parties.

Both parties sign and date. That's it. You can't get more basic than that, but it can work as well as a five-page sales contract. If both parties wish to go through with the agreement, you don't need anything else. If one party wants out, even a five-page contract can be difficult to enforce with good lawyers.

You can write up a sales contract in just a few lines and it will be valid as long as you include these items and both parties sign.

(A close variation of the example above was used to buy a great property; I wouldn't recommend it, but in my case it was called for, because the seller was a lot more anxious to sell than I was to buy, and the settlement date was fairly close. It turned out to be a wonderful deal.)

There are many ways to find loopholes. I try to make the loopholes very small for the seller. The one thing I am always interested in is that if the seller changes his/her mind after hearing of the potential value of the property from me, I want to make sure I can make the seller go through with the sale. Therefore, I might give a bit more attention to the contract than the outline above.

Plus, it must be mentioned that many settlements have problems. A settlement is the time when legal ownership changes hands and payment is made. No matter what legal advice you get, there's no guarantee it will go smoothly because there are always new issues that your attorney has never had. For example, at the first house we ever sold, the purchaser's moving truck arrived three hours early, shortly before the late-morning scheduled settlement. To be nice, I said they could start moving in so they wouldn't have to pay for extra movers' time. Well, settlement didn't go through because of an objection by a neighbor, and while it took six weeks to work out, the purchasers were in our house, we were out and not getting paid, and there was nothing we could do. Do you think we ever did that again?

The most important aspect to include in a sales contract, as far as I am concerned, is the legal right to go through with the purchase, but also to allow as much time as possible to inspect the property, without losing a dime. You need this time to come up with a way to pay for it and to make it work if you go through with the purchase. If you can get one or two months of time, you can perhaps find tenants for part of the space, find creative financing, or in other ways figure out a way to make it work. There is no better feeling than to find a great studio and to have tenants signed and paid before you need to put in your money and take possession.

Always give yourself a back escape door. The way to do this so that the seller doesn't think you are just too poor to afford the property is to base the delay of settlement on the need to properly inspect the building. It is normal to bring in experts to go over the structure and to look for defects and hazardous conditions. This is acceptable, and the language for this should be that you will have a period of time (try to get 30 to 60 days) to inspect the property and the right to terminate the agreement - <u>at purchaser's sole discretion</u> – and to have any deposit returned. If you need more time, you can also write into the sales contract that you have the right to give a non-refundable deposit of ($_____) to extend the inspection period.   If you are serious about taking a building, it may be worth it to risk a couple thousand dollars (or more). If you go through with the sale, the deposit will be credited towards the purchase price. If you bail out, the deposit you forfeit may be small compared to the losses you will incur by taking procession of a bad property.

Even if nothing is wrong with the building, but you have just changed your mind about buying it, you will have the right to terminate the deal.   Never, ever, get yourself into a deal without having this option for at least two weeks. It is your time to make a sober assessment of what your emotions or 'desperate need to find a studio' feelings may have suppressed.

Another clause that is common to find in purchase contracts concerns financing. Few people pay cash for a building, so it is common to have a clause that says that the sale is contingent on securing within (60) days, bank financing of (75)% at (9)% over (20) years (sample numbers in parentheses).

In many cases, the owner may want your financial statement to see if you would even qualify for a bank mortgage.   But remember, it's been my experience that when dealing with old properties, and by giving the impression up front that I can do the deal 'if I want to,' it is more a matter of whether the building will qualify for a bank mortgage. In other words, try not to get backed into a corner. I also find that agents seem more anxious to find out the financial ability of the purchaser in order to protect their clients (agents in many cases work for the seller), but rarely have I been asked to show a financial statement by an owner selling directly without the aid of an agent. The idea of checking is that agents and sellers don't want to tie up a property, then turn away other prospective purchasers only to find out that the deal can't go through because a bank won't lend you the money. For the type of property you will be looking for, I doubt if there will be many people standing in line to make purchase offers. As a last resort, offer a financial statement only after the inspection period. Perhaps you can find a partner by then.

Obviously, all cash gets you a better deal. Remember, though, that "all cash" is to the seller; it doesn't mean that you won't get bank financing, only that the seller is not taking back any loans. The seller expects to be paid in full at settlement, and how you come up with the money is your business.

You can almost always negotiate the best deal by offering to the seller all cash in a short time. It will also get the owner's attention the fastest. That is the way to begin your negotiations. A bit later and before you sign a deal, or even after the deal has been signed and you are in the free inspection period, you can begin to wiggle out and say that bank financing is taking longer than expected (not your fault, of course) or that the inspectors want to take a closer look at a few items, but that all will work out if you can only have a few more weeks of the option. Buying yourself time this way while keeping the property locked in might be the only alternative. It might not be 100% fair to the seller, but the seller can make his/her own decision. Remember, this is a game of bluff, and it doesn't always work. If the owner calls your bluff and you don't lock in at the end of the inspection deadline, you can lose the deal.

If you discover 'problems' with the property, you might be able to renegotiate the signed deal (which you could always back out of in any case) to win more time or more concessions. One idea might be to then negotiate a one-year lease, with an option to buy, but with some of your payments going against the purchase price. Another option is getting the owner to take back some financing.

Don't be intimidated by the seller. Sellers come in all types. Often they are owners of businesses or have inherited their property and they are not thinking of the potential of the real estate. Remember also, often the owner thinks that you are the sucker, for wanting an old, run-down building that no one has looked at in months or years.

For future use, in case you want to sell the building and move to a larger studio building. If you use an agent to sell a building, do not be afraid to modify a boilerplate listing agreement as well. I always cross out the part about having the broker get part or all of a purchaser's deposit if the purchaser defaults. I only allow the broker to get the agreed-upon percentage if the settlement occurs and the property is transferred. I don't want the broker/agent to collect money on a sale unless the sale goes through; it's their job to find the seller a qualified purchaser who will go through with the settlement. Also, don't sign listing agreements for longer than ninety days; if the agent is doing a good job, you can always extend the period.

AFTER SIGNED AGREEMENT, BUT BEFORE SETTLEMENT

There are many things that have to be done quickly the minute a deal has been signed and before you lose a dime. You might have ten days, or you might have ninety days, but you will have to move quickly.

Read this entire book first. Important items discussed under construction, for example, have to be considered before you purchase the space.

Inspect. Get a good, professional inspector and go over the roof, structure, heating, air conditioning, plumbing, electrical system, and any item inside, outside, under it or over it that may affect the property and cost you money. Especially ask about hazardous wastes, asbestos, and heating tanks. You will be forming some ideas about how to use the building, so then go and talk to electrical, plumbing and heating contractors. They will give you an idea of what it will cost to do what you want - and their estimates are free. Along the way, you get an awful lot of information.

One hint is to ask the building inspector for recommendations on hiring someone. Occasionally, inspectors themselves will do work on the side. Or they recommend someone who used to be an inspector. There's nothing like hiring someone who really knows the community's codes, and perhaps personally knows the current inspector and what attitude that person might use to enforced the building codes. Sometimes they are willing to overlook some gray areas if the bulk of the work is satisfactory to them. That is because any fix-up of an old building is better than keeping it in its present state.

Building Codes. In any case, you will need to discuss the property and any code violations and/or zoning problems for the use you intend to give it. You can also go to the county/city office and talk to the building inspector. Be careful and non-committal when talking. Ask about the building but be vague about your use. Try not to use terms like 'contemporary sculpture.' This is not the time to educate the public about art. 'A small design shop' might be a better description to use. What you are really there for is to find out what the building might be used for, from the city's point of view, and if there are any problems that it might have. Indicate that you don't want to do any remodeling now, and you want to know if it can be used 'as is.' Talk in terms of making a few 'repairs.' If you indicate that you will be renovating the property, the city will ask that everything be brought up to code, and that is something that could cost you more than you might want to pay. Often I've found that the soft approach works, and that improvements can be made slowly without kicking in a 'total renovation' rating. Usually, artists do a lot of cosmetic improvements, such as new paint, partitions (not structural walls), and floor covering. These items should not be a concern to the governmental codes and you need not mention them. Stick to the structural, fire, electrical and plumbing issues.

In large cities, you will have to go to various counters because each inspector specializes in a certain area: electrical, plumbing, zoning, fire, elevator, building/structural, signage, and possibly others. When you submit blueprints, each has to sign off on the plans as well as do a field inspection.

For Public Use. If you want to have public activities and build into the building a performance space or exhibition space, you will have to modify it for public use. Generally, attention is paid to the number of exits, fire pulls and fire alarm systems, sprinklers, handicapped access, fire covering on walls and ceilings, hallway plans, and there will be more issues mentioned once you talk to the building inspector. The good part is that if you are taking over a single building, most of this public use activity will probably take place on the ground floor where it is easier to satisfy the building code demands.

Historic Designation: Some old buildings might already be designated as historic properties. In most cases, however, industrial property is just old but not considered historically interesting. You may be able to change that, if you desire. The warehouses, stables, and manufacturing plants from the turn of the twentieth century are filled with history and easily could be designated. The question then becomes, so what?

Usually, owners of designated properties can be eligible for additional tax write-offs. The values of these write-offs have declined in recent years. You may be able to get special designated loans, but these loans, which will demand additional architectural plans, administrative and overall work, as well as paying prevailing wages, may in fact cost you more than if you just did the work by paying the lowest- bidding contractor. The designation may also limit what you do.

Generally speaking, artists taking over old properties are not looking to make a dramatic change to the outside. Keeping the historic look is the easiest way to go, because it costs money to make changes. You can almost always do what you want inside, in any case, unless you are involved with an historic renovation program. I don't advise you go this way, with one exception. If you have a really big deal that will involve either investors or big government grants, you may find this pays. But if you read the last segment about artists' buildings, you may also agree that it might not be a worthwhile goal or a satisfying end result.

If you want to learn more about historic

designation, by all means contact the local and state historic commissions. The National Trust for Historic Preservation (800-944-6847 or nationaltrust.org) can help you locate the appropriate agencies.

Zoning. Find out how the property is zoned. All properties are zoned for particular uses, and all communitics have uses that are permitted under that specific zoning. You can also talk to the zoning inspector. Doing this in a big city is a lot more difficult than in a small city or town, where thc building inspector probably knows every building one by one. In a large city, thc zoning inspector will probably just go by the book.

For zoning questions, you should go through the same vague, non-committal chitchat about what might be allowed. Normally, properties are zoned for residential, industrial or commercial use. Then there are special categories, such as farm, school, wetland, airport district, etc. Within these groups, there are levels. For example, there could be light industrial and heavy industrial (art studios often are considered light industrial); under residential, there could be single-family dwellings and multi-family apartmcnt buildings. Each zoning classification then has specific uses. They may mention such business as gas stations, retail stores, theaters, etc. You will rarely find art studios. Expect that the building and/or zoning officers know almost nothing about art studios. Find out what would be allowed, and see how many categories you can fit into. An art studio just may come under a generic heading of office and warehouse.

The ticklish item is to deal with living. First you need to determine if the zoning allows residential use. Then you need to find out if building codes allow both residential and 'studio work' under the same roof.

The surprise is that you may find there are old laws on the books that no one knows about. When I came to North Adams, I followed up on a hunch and discovered I was right. In the old days, there always used to be a 'watchman' living in a small apartment in the mill; or in other buildings, the proprietors would have an apartment above the business. The zoning rules allowed this living, and in many communities no one ever changed the rules.

Actually, all the zoning and building codes were in the process of being modernized and overhauled when I came, but I was able to get in before they were officially changed. Once in, you become 'grandfathered' and they can't kick you out or make you stop what you had permission to do before the law was changed. Someone else buying another mill building today would not receive the same permit. However, my permit would transfer to someone buying my building if that person wanted to continue the same use. This is true in most places in this country.

Again, always ask in a way that gives the impression that you are just inquiring. You don't want to push any buttons, yet. But you do need to find out if there will be any problem carrying out your work in this location, and you should think about all possible activities that you may want to do sometime in the future.

Insurance, Taxes. Call around and get two or three quotes for property insurance. Also find out the taxes and what the appraised value is. You want rates for enough insurance so that, if the building burns down, you come out whole. In addition to fire and liability insurance, you may need title insurance, which is arranged before settlement. This protects you if anyone makes a claim on your property. With old properties, you never know who may come out of the woodwork and claim they own it. If you have a mortgage, the bank probably will insist upon it.

Closing Costs. You also need to know what the closing costs will be. What the purchaser and what the seller pay should have been determined in the sales agreement. You will need an attorney to help you settle. The fee might be around $500 to $1,000 to do the complete settlement, including recording the title. The lawyer might also be able to help you with zoning issues. Again, you can get the estimates without paying anything, subject to the deal going through. In some states, you need to pay transfer taxes and recording fees. Whether you or the seller pays these fees is up to how you negotiate the deal.

Settlement is customarily held either in a bank or at a lawyer's office. Usually papers have to be signed, witnessed and notarized, and someone has to make an accounting of the money. There might be a credit to one of the parties for money owed or money already paid for taxes or some utilities. For example, if the owner has paid the taxes through the year, and when you take ownership there are two months left of the tax year, then you have to reimburse the owner for the months that he has already paid for and which you will really owe upon owning the property.

Utilities. Call the utility companies (unless the owner has supplied you with old bills) and try to find out the usage history. You might become less enthusiastic when you find out how much it costs to heat a large space through the winter. One large heating system may have so much cost associated with its operation that you will have to rent out spaces to justify its use. Several heating systems will allow you to mothball some of the building. Find out about water usage as well.

History and Hazardous Wastes. Get the history of the building. When you go to the public records office to find the previous purchase price, existing mortgages and taxes due, also find out whether the city has any concerns. There might be a record of spills and hazardous waste cleanups. Find out what was produced or done at the property. Be equally concerned and observant about the outside area. Could there be hazardous wastes in the ground? Are there oily spots on the floor? Be a detective.

PCB (Polychlorinated Biphenyl) is a cancer-causing oil that was used in electrical transformers and for many other things. It can be found in stains and wet areas inside and out, but most common would be to find working transformers that have PCB in them. Although there is a huge political debate about it – as there was about asbestos – it nevertheless can bankrupt you if you are forced to clean it up. Some owners will suddenly sound very fuzzy to you when you ask about this. (Ask after you have a signed agreement but before you lock into losing a deposit, unless you can't come to a deal; then try to mention your concerns to indicate the problems the owner will keep if transfer of the property is not made.)

The main problems, other than special

manufacturing wastes, will be pipe, boiler and floor asbestos, transformers with PCB oil, and buried oil tanks. Read about asbestos under the construction section of the book. Get an estimate to remove all of the pipe and boiler asbestos insulation, and plan what to do with the floor. PCB transformers can be kept if they are not leaking, but sooner or later you will pay to have them removed.

If you have a buried heating oil tank, have a pressure test done. Also, make sure that in the sales agreement, the former owner maintains legal responsibility for this potential expense. If the tank has leaked, it can cost you easily $50,000 to clean it up. So don't take it lightly.

Knowing the 'Day-After' Costs Before. I always want to know, the day I take ownership of a property, what I will face. Do I need to cut the grass, clean out the gutters, or repair a leak? Do I need to sweep out the building, pick up trash, or figure out how to set the thermostats to prevent freezing? As the settlement day approaches, obviously I will have made arrangements with the utility companies to have active accounts, but all of this adds up to time and cash going out. Finally, I need to figure out what has to be done before I move in, and in the case of an art studio, how easy the move will be.

Doing a Budget. Forget the accounting programs in your computer for a moment; just get a piece of paper and scribble down the costs as best as you can guess. A few days later, add items you've forgotten about and go through the numbers again. For each item – and I mean basic ones like electrical work, plumbing and heating, walls, painting, doors and hardware, etc., I usually do a high and a low figure - like the best-case and worst-case amounts. Then add it all up. The total may scare you at first. But don't get glassy-eyed about the costs - they are rarely lower than you expect, especially the first time you do a building renovation.

Getting the Word Out. When all is said and done, you have a totally new picture of whether this is a 'deal' or not. It can take your breath away. But in truth, if you look at all the items, and you still think it makes sense, you might just have a deal of a lifetime.

I also need to know, when I go into a deal, if I could make money by selling (flipping) the property to someone else quickly. That means that I have found a bargain. A bargain is a bargain, whether it's something you have found at a yard sale or an old building you've found among the thousands of buildings in the region. Just as one person's trash is another's treasure, the owner probably doesn't know the value of the property to the art market. At the same time, other artists probably never thought about the value of a property that could be converted to arts use, even if they walked by that building day after day. I have always found satisfaction in knowing that once I 'announce' my pending purchase (only after it is locked up with a written sales agreement) to art friends, there is so much demand that I could easily walk away with a profit if I wanted. This is especially important if you need to rent out space. The reaction from your artist friends about the property will give you an idea whether your rental plans are feasible.

The following is a checklist of things to consider. Mark down whether you need to get more information, whether the item needs lots of work, versus something that can get by for a while, or something that is fine as is. Also, read the construction section of this book to get a better idea of what has to be done. This list is what I carry in my head all the time, whenever I look at potential studio space. After reading the rest of the book, you will know more about these items. It does not take a professional to get an idea of what a potential building might involve. Only after you have a signed purchase agreement do you then have to have a more detailed estimate of what it will take to deal with each item, either on your immediate list or on your long-term list.

Put in any kind of grading system you want - letter grades, one to ten, or whatever you like. The point is to get a handle on each item and see which ones stand out as likely deal breakers.

Always ask yourself this question: "If I lose or turn down the building, will I regret it? " But be prepared to pass for non-emotional reasons. It may be a dream studio in a dream location at a dream (low) price, but if there is a hazardous-waste issue, for example, that could cost you

Property Inspection Check List	Can-Get- By/OK	Some-Patching	Major-Problem
Structure			
Roof			
Windows			
Electrical			
Plumbing			
Heating-a/c			
Floors			
Walls			
Asbestos			
Underground tanks			
Hazardous wastes			
Exterior skin			
Exterior yard			
Fire systems			
Access			
Exits, emerg. lights			
Lights			
Sewer, Water			
Hot water			
Bathrooms			
Elevator			
Insulation			
Cleaning			
	Good	So-So	Bad
Location convenience			
Zoning			
Code violations			
Value			
Potential of neighborhood			
Safety			
Potential for commercial			
Potential for sub-leasing			
Potential for broader arts use			
City appraisal			
Taxes			
Insurance rate			
Electrical use			
Gas/heat use			
Maintenance upkeep			
Trash service			
Beauty of building			
Does it need a lot of work?			

$200,000, maybe you should consider the deal a 'pass.' There will be another opportunity in the future. Most people make mistakes in buying property when they think it's the only chance they will have. In the stock market, cheap stocks can still go down. On the other hand, timing is everything in real estate, and when you have a bargain, grab it. Show it to your friends once you have the property locked in; like a hot style in your art, you'll know if it's a great deal by their reactions.

CHAPTER 3
Money Matters

The main way to lower the amount you have to pay is to find a way for someone else to pay it.

Money is the problem, or should I say the lack of it. I know some artists who, by birth or marriage, do not need to worry about the costs of a studio. But for most of us, it is the one concern and limitation for realizing our dreams. There are ways to deal with these limitations.

I am always quietly shocked at how artists seem to come up with money to buy a photographer's time to shoot slides of their work, and yet do not take that money to buy better studio space. My advice is to learn to take your own slides, and use the savings to make better art in a more productive space.

RENTING

In a situation where renting is a must, you might be able to reduce the pain. Other than rent reductions, you should look at it as either a fantastic opportunity to concentrate purely on art, or a short-term situation while you look around for something better. If you have a great rental deal that you think will last for a while, then it might pay to do some fix-up work and make it as functional as you can.

Just as most 22-year-olds might not feel that they can commit themselves to buying houses, once married they might change their tunes. Being an artist is like a marriage - and there are few divorces.

Bartering. I must recommend reading my book The Art World Dream, because it gives a number of concepts to pursue income and still stay on a professional arts course. In addition to the obvious ways of earning money through an outside job, art sales, or teaching, I know artists who rent studios and then pay less by having various responsibilities in the building. One friend in the Boston area (Cambridge) has 1,000 square feet free, by making himself available to work in his landlord's furniture store, located in the same building, most Saturdays (but since he is on standby, he can still do his artwork) and a few hours during the week. This saves him $500 in rent (already a bargain for that area).

Most artists' buildings need upkeep, but their landlords cannot afford traditional maintenance services. Bartering is a perfect way of getting the rent down to your budget.

Fixing Up the Space. Many owners of large, run-down buildings do not have the wherewithal to do the renovation themselves. Even in my studio building, I am too busy to get involved with each studio improvement. If a prospective or existing tenant comes to me and proposes a solid improvement, I will often fund the material costs if the tenant will do the labor. By sharing expenses, we both get a bargain. By funding the improvement, I am investing in my own property and giving the tenant an incentive to do the labor that he/she might not agree to do if he/she also had to pay for the materials. Sometimes I will lower the rent for a period of time to offset additional improvements by a tenant. The tenant locks in the rent, but the initial months' payments go to paying for materials. Hopefully, the improvements will allow me to raise the rent for the next tenant, while we both feel that we are getting a 50% discount on the project.

Usually a building permit does not need to be pulled for tenant's improvements, since they often involve non-structural partitions, loft structures, and other decorating items. If electrical work has to be done, I use a licensed electrician who knows whether to get a permit or not; simple replacements and repairs do not usually need one.

Other Arrangements. It is difficult to describe all the different kinds of arrangements that can be made, but in my many years of dealing with studio space, I've found that in the majority of cases there is room for a special deal. Most studios are in old properties, and by their very nature there is some reason why they are in the state they are. Artists can satisfy their rent demands in ways other than with dollars. Especially during tough times, there may be an opportunity to work it through with the landlord. Sharing space and pooling resources offers more options. Getting several months' free rent while the space is being 'improved' is another way.

PURCHASE

If a purchase is made, then instead of paying rent, assuming you borrowed money for the property, you are making monthly payments on the mortgage. The money goes for the interest on the loan as well as to pay off the loan. If all goes well, the mortgage payment plus insurance and taxes (which in most rental cases are paid by the landlord) won't be any higher than a rent payment. It could be a lot less.

What Does It Cost Monthly? Big studios will cost. But a purchase will not necessarily cost you more than renting. You can use a mortgage amortization calculator and get a payment schedule online at various sites (usually a free service at brokers' and banks' sites; search for "Mortgage Amortization"). Plug in the loan amount, interest rate and term, and they will provide you with a breakdown. If you are not online, you can go to most banks' mortgage departments and ask if they have a mortgage calculator or amortization schedule.

If you have little patience for reading the explanation below, you can generally estimate that your monthly obligation will be about 1% of the building's cost. So if you are purchasing a $100,000 building and ideally want a mortgage to cover the entire amount, the monthly mortgage payment will be roughly $1,000 (and probably a bit less with today's low interest rates).

I have a little paperback book of charts that I received before the Internet was in operation, to which I still refer. Each page has a different interest rate, and on each page to one side are the dollar amounts and at the top are years. So, for example, if you look at the 9% chart, and look to the left to find $100,000 and at the top to find 20 years, for example, it will show that the monthly mortgage amount of principal and interest will be $899.73. At 7%, the monthly payment will be $775.30.

The amount of the principal will change in relation to the amount of interest, in order to keep the monthly payment the same during the life of the mortgage. In the beginning, you are paying interest on the entire $100,000, so very little of your payment goes to pay off the principal. In fact, during the first few years, roughly $2,000 out of more than $10,000 of your annual payments will go to pay down the principal. The $8,000 goes just for interest. But as you slowly pay it down, you gradually pay less in interest and more in principal. During the later years, most of your monthly payment goes towards principal.

At 9%, $899.73 multiplied by 240 months (20 years) equals $215,935.20, of which only $100,000 is the original loan amount. At 7%, your total payments will equal $186,072.00, a reduction of almost $30,000 for a difference in interest of just two percentage points. It pays to find the lowest interest rate on a loan.

You end up paying so much interest that, if you shorten the mortgage to fifteen years, for example, you will save an impressive amount of money.

If the loan term is only fifteen years, your monthly payment will be higher - at 7%, it will be $898.83, and at 9 %, it will be $1,014.27.

However, at 9%, your total payments will equal $182,568.60. By paying just $114.54 more per month at 9%, you will save $33,366.60 over the course of the loan and save five years of making payments.

The real reward is that after fifteen years you will not have to make monthly mortgage payments, saving yourself the $1,014.27 monthly headache. This money can then be used for making art.

If you can push your monthly payment a bit higher, it pays. It used to be encouraged to take a 30-year mortgage to minimize your monthly payment. This was good advice if you were planning on selling the property in a few years. If you have a substantial building, my guess is that you will be holding on to it for quite some time. Your goal should be to set up your rentals so that they can cover your debt amount that is set for no more than fifteen years.

Loan Amortization:
(7, 8, 9% interest; 15 & 20 years)

Loan Amount: $100,000 Interest Rate: 7% Years: 15
Monthly Principal & Interest:	$898.83
Total Number of Payments:	180
Total of 180 Payments:	$161,789.09
Original Loan Amount:	$100,000.00
Total Interest Paid:	$61,789.09

Loan Amount: $100,000 Interest Rate: 7% Years: 20
Monthly Principal & Interest:	$775.30
Total Number of Payments:	240
Total of 240 Payments:	$186,071.74
Original Loan Amount:	$100,000.00
Total Interest Paid:	$86,071.74

Loan Amount: $100,000 Interest Rate: 8% Years: 15
Monthly Principal & Interest:	$955.65
Total Number of Payments:	180
Total of 180 Payments:	$172,017.38
Original Loan Amount:	$100,000.00
Total Interest Paid:	$72,017.38

Loan Amount: $100,000 Interest Rate: 8% Years: 20
Monthly Principal & Interest:	$836.44
Total Number of Payments:	240
Total of 240 Payments:	$200,745.62
Original Loan Amount:	$100,000.00
Total Interest Paid:	$100,745.62

Loan Amount: $100,000 Interest Rate: 9% Years: 15
Monthly Principal & Interest:	$1,014.27
Total Number of Payments:	180
Total of 180 Payments:	$182,567.99
Original Loan Amount:	$100,000.00
Total Interest Paid:	$82,567.99

Loan Amount: $100,000 Interest Rate: 9% Years: 20
Monthly Principal & Interest:	$899.73
Total Number of Payments:	240
Total of 240 Payments:	$215,934.23
Original Loan Amount:	$100,000.00
Total Interest Paid:	$115,934.23

On Top of the Mortgage. Just as in renting, you still need to figure in utility expenses. But as owner, you also need to pay for building insurance, water and sewer, and real-estate taxes. Plus, if you had to put cash down at the time of the purchase, even though you don't have to make rent payments, you are losing whatever the money might have brought to you in income if you had invested it. For example, if you put $10,000 down, had you invested this amount and gotten a 6% return, you would be losing annual income of $600. You don't feel it directly, but it's there. If you had to borrow the down payment in a second loan, then, of course, you would need to add this amount to your monthly nut.

Add up all these expenses to your mortgage payments, and you get the real cost of owning property, exclusive of maintenance and improvements.

How to Lower the Monthly Nut. The main way to lower the amount you have to pay is to find a way for someone else to pay it. The obvious answer is to rent out a portion of your space.

It goes without saying that, when you rent or buy quantity, you should get a discount. So, when you rent smaller spaces, tenants should pay more. It is possible to rent out just one half of your building and get sufficient income to pay for all of your expenses.

Other ways include doing activities that will bring in additional income, but they entail work. For example, can you use part of the space as a gallery, which you either run or rent out for individual shows; can you partner some of the space in return for things that you normally pay for? Can a carpenter use the space and save you the expense of making stretchers, making repairs, or fixing up the building as part of the deal? Can you do community projects and get grants to help subsidize the projects as well as your space? And obviously, combining your space with living, and thus save paying for a separate residential rental, is a way many artists justify larger buildings.

Financing a Purchase. Looking for someone to lend you the money for an old property is an art in itself. Generally, you will need to go to several banks. Although it's ironic, you can get money out of bankers if they are convinced that you don't need it. If they think you really need the loan, they will turn you down. Why? Because they want to know, above anything else, if you have other income or assets to satisfy the loan amount should your business fail. Savvy investors will ask the same questions that banks will.

Do a financial plan; it's not that difficult. Project your monthly expenses and your monthly income. Lenders simply want to know if your income will cover all your building expenses, including their loan.   Try to project five years into the future; you should show rents increasing at a faster rate than your estimated expenses. Always be realistic, but in your own figures be conservative; in the figures you show the bank or investor, be positive. For your income, it is common to include a vacancy factor of 5%, for example. Privately, plan on not renting all the spaces for a while and see what happens to your profits and losses.

The idea of using an investor is to have someone with assets, in whom a bank would be willing to invest money. The loan will still be tied to the property, but will have a personal guarantee by someone the bank trusts.

One bank or investor may not be willing to lend you enough money. You might have to put together a package that will include some bank loans, some city grants, some private investors, and some seller financing.

Bank Financing. The ideal purchase is to have the bank lending you the money. The main disadvantage of buying a commercial property is that the bank cannot give you a residential mortgage, which carries much lower rates and requires less cash down.

Banks require you to have good income as well as sufficient assets (they won't take artworks as assets unless you can show how well they sold at Sotheby's), even though the real estate becomes the main asset they attach. By federal regulation, they can't give you a 100% loan, at least not in obvious ways. I've gotten around this by attaching a renovation schedule. Say, for example, I want to purchase a building for $50,000, and I want to spend an additional $50,000 fixing up the property. I give the bank a detail list (based on estimates), and ask for a $75,000 acquisition and renovation loan. If they give me the loan, I've just gotten $25,000 over the purchase amount, although I've also obligated myself to doing a lot of renovation. However, the trick now is to do the $50,000 worth of work for $25,000. The banks don't follow the details as well, and I can usually swing it for less. In addition, I've bought myself working time, so that by the time I am half-way through the $50,000 renovation (having only used the $25,000), I can rent out space (which hopefully was pre-rented on condition of fixing up the space) and use that income to finish doing the building. I can't tell you that you can do this or if this would work, but occasionally there is some room to fudge, especially for small projects. Believe me, you will qualify as a 'small loan.'

There are fewer ways to get around having a good income statement. If your spouse works, and your combined incomes seem sufficient, you might be able to get by. If you've had an unusually good year selling work, you can bend the numbers to show the income without necessarily showing all the expenses. Usually the bank's income and expense forms, which they ask you to fill out, requests information about all your income and set, monthly expenses. So the cost of making art doesn't have to be included, unless they ask specifically.

Determining how good you are as a customer or potential borrower can affect the interest rate. Some banks have flexibility to some degree. As with everything, always ask if they can make it lower. In addition to the interest rate, banks will try to charge you points to be paid at settlement. A point is equal to 1% of the loan. Try to avoid points if you can.

Talk to bankers, and if they expose weak spots, try to do a better job with another bank. Also tell them how much of a community service they will be performing if they lend you money for an old building in a bad neighborhood that will be converted to arts use. Tell them your big plans, for community art classes for children, exhibitions, school tours, and helping the region's art community as well. It won't hurt. Above all, be well versed in your profit and loss projections.

Finally, although it is more difficult for commercial properties, try to search online for loans. It is also a quick way to find out the weaknesses in your applications.

Partners. In addition to what you can put together, you could try to bring in partners to co-sign loan applications. But beware. Marriages where two people love each other more often than not break apart. You just may be stuck with your worst nightmare. Plus, the old saying goes that friends and business don't mix.

If you are certain that this is your only route, try to keep majority (51%) control of the project, and look for escape doors. Try to build in a buy-out option so that, for any reason, you can buy out your partner. It works much better if you use a partnership as a temporary financing bandage and not as a long-term merger.

Despite all the possible problems, getting a group of artists to go in with you is still a viable answer, especially when the purchase is ambitious and your resources are limited. However, even a group of artists may not help much with bankers. They want someone substantial to go after when all else fails.

Commercial Condominium. This route is probably too complicated to do at first. It is a way to cash in down the line, when your building is full of tenants and you desire to sell their portions to them. The only way it works at the early stages is to take a property, divide it up, and offer to sell pieces outright to others. In essence, you are just buying a part of the building for your own use, which, of course, lowers your obligation. The real trick is to sell the other portions for an amount that will allow you to get your space for nearly nothing. If you have a great bargain and enough time before you need to settle, you may be able to swing it. In a sense it is like a partnership, but you may want to have additional legal documents permanently dividing up the building. There are complications because of common areas, roof, mechanical systems, etc. Some buildings work better than others.

Keep in mind that if this type of arrangement works in the beginning, then it should work later. Don't rush into it just because you think it's a fast way to reduce the money you need. If the property is such a good deal that you can attract tenants and investors so quickly, you might do better a year or two from now. Think of yourself as a wholesaler, looking to sell some goods retail. If the goods don't have a short shelf life, you might be better off taking your time to find the best retail price you can get.

Legal condominium documents are complicated and expensive to prepare, and should be entered into with care. If you do go this route, try not to have someone draw them up from scratch. Many years ago it cost $25,000 to have them prepared for a small building. Today, with so many commercial condos out there, you should be able to find documents to copy and then just customize them to fit your use.

Seller Financing. The better deal is for the sellers to take back financing. Often they realize that it is the only way to get rid of an old building. They should offer financing that is competitive with what a bank would give. After all, they know their buildings, and as long as they have received some money as a down payment, they are much better off than keeping the property empty and paying taxes and insurance on it. In addition, if they have owned the property for a long time, they have already depreciated it on their taxes and they will owe Uncle Sam a substantial capital-gains tax on the sale. By taking back financing, they will only pay tax on the money actually collected.

Family. I've known many artists who are too proud to get money from 'home.' To my mind, if money is available from a source and it is to be put to good use and you will be using it to create art, why deny yourself just because you think you won't feel 'independent?' Borrow from home by all means. If your goal of being an artist is to show your family how you can hold your own, you are missing the point. Besides, you should be able to repay it just as if it were a bank loan. For me, being an artist means making the greatest art I know how to do. (Of course, I define what great art is.)

City and State Grants and Loans. Many cities and regions have quasi public-private not-for-profit entities (some are called Community Development Corporations), whose purpose is to loan money to new businesses to stimulate the local economy and create jobs. They often grant loans that bankers feel present too much risk.

There are also grants, especially if you partner your purchase with a community program or historic renovations. When my wife and I took over the Beaver Mill, we promised as much. By starting the Berkshire School of Contemporary Art, or Contemporary Artists Center, we satisfied the owner's (the mill was owned by a community organization) condition that by selling us the mill, we would continue to benefit the community in some way. Another exception was during the renovation of a downtown property. The city had a grant program to use for facade work; since I was going to paint the exterior and repair the broken windows anyway, this grant came in handy to lower my costs and it didn't involve much from me.

Generally, I've never been a fan of using public money for real-estate projects because the paper headaches are usually not worth what you get in return. However, there are exceptions, and when no other answer appears, look everywhere for money.

Internal Sources. I've observed too many artists who want a better studio but say they can't afford it. In half of the cases, that is simply not true. They can't afford the studio of their dreams because they just bought a new car, for example. Artists waste money on lots of things that I would never dream of spending on. They will spend hundreds of dollars for slides, or for making a brochure of their work, or for designing a web site, or for business cards, or for having someone else make their stretchers and frames. They will spend as carelessly for personal items as well.

I don't want to preach or tell artists how to live, but I can tell them that if they are as serious about their art as they claim, then they'd better rethink their priorities.

Sit down and write down your entire budget. It might be possible to reallocate income and reduce expenses for more effective use. It might also be more economical when viewed as a five-year plan rather than as spending money on a day-to-day basis.

CHAPTER 4
Legal Matters

Being a creator is still atypical in the business world.

Now that you have found a studio and dealt with the money end to figure out how to pay for it, there are several legal issues to deal with.

Are you buying an individual property or a commercial condominium? Will you be leasing out spaces to others? Who will be the legal owner?

As with several items in this book, I am giving you information based largely on experience. Many lawyers reading this would cringe. Consult with your lawyer, because only he/she knows your specific situation. Hopefully, the information I am passing on to you will give you some background material and some ideas for getting a better advantage.

OWNERSHIP

Who Should Buy the Studio Property? The idea of great studio spaces is to buy quantity, then sublet part of it to pay the bulk of the costs of owning the property. Usually, the best way to do this is to offer a lease to artist-tenants or commercial tenants. However, we will discuss in whose name the property should be legally owned: whether by you as an individual, or as a corporation or partnership. Then this legal entity can enter into leases with tenants. It might also come to pass that someday, rather than selling the entire building as a whole, you might want to sell part of it in the form of a commercial condominium or as a commercial cooperative, depending on the size. Hopefully, in the sales agreement, you put under "Purchaser" your name, plus "in the name of an entity to be formed." This allows you flexibility until you settle.

Lessor's Name. Setting up a new name for the owner is best if you intend to rent spaces to other artists - not only for legal protection and tax advantages, but also for marketing. Tenants, especially artists, resent writing rent checks payable to your personal name. Emotionally, they don't realize that you are not taking their checks and putting them into your pockets to enjoy, but you have your own money obligations that may be more pressing than theirs. Having the rent checks made out to an impersonal company name minimizes some of these feelings.

Sole Proprietor. This is where you legally own the property in your own name. As a business, you can still deduct expenses through a Schedule C form on your federal taxes. The main disadvantage is that if anything should happen, a lawsuit may be brought against you individually. The advantage of buying a property this way is that you don't have to legally set up anything. But if you rent out space to other artists, there is a host of potential problems to give pause for this type of ownership.

Limited Partnership. This is a legal entity that allows you to have partners who share in the losses and profits, as well as the tax write-offs, of a property. If you set it up this way, you can be the general partner with all the authority to run it the way you want. The limited partners are silent, passive investors only. The general partner has the liability, while the silent partners are just investors and don't share any liability.

Corporation. A corporation is a legal entity that can conduct business and own property. Corporations can have private or public stock. While it is possible to take an aggressive stand about art expenses on a Schedule C form, a corporation allows you to deduct additional expenses. Plus, and this is informal advice, the IRS tends to let a lot more pass by for corporations than it does for individuals. That is because companies normally pay for employees to travel on business, purchase supplies, and have other costs associated with running the business that are not questioned as closely as if, for example, you were claiming travel expenses on your personal tax return using a Schedule C form. They assume that no one is personally profiting from the corporation's business affairs.

I am not advocating doing anything wrong, but there has been a history of the IRS questioning whether an artist's deductions for expenses are legitimate when the artist didn't earn a profit. Although there is less of that now, being a creator is still atypical in the business world.

A corporate entity makes your business seem more in keeping with other companies. It also allows you to deduct medical insurance, for example. It makes it easier to set up payroll for employees and it treats expenses in a more straightforward manner. In general, I would consider a corporation for your studio operations as well as for real estate, but your attorney should advise you. There are ownership and estate issues involved as well.

The most important aspect of a corporation is that it provides significant personal protection in case of a lawsuit or bankruptcy, without devastating your personal assets. However, you won't have this protection if you, as a corporate officer, don't pay federal taxes, payroll, and payroll taxes, to mention a few things.

In the case of owning property, if your best laid plans fail, a corporation will limit your liabilities. Since you can own 100% of the stock, it will not affect your ability to take out income from profits.

See your tax accountant and/or lawyer for more details and advice before deciding.

Tax Aspects. As you can see, corporations give you some advantages in claiming deductions. If you own an old building that is being converted to studio use, you will probably need an accountant, at least to file year-end taxes.

Certainly, there are some additional filings and taxes to pay. Corporations are required to file annual tax returns, and some state and federal taxes are required. You will also have some legal expenses in setting up the corporation and perhaps in maintaining it. For example, the annual meeting notices and annual reports must be sent in each year. However, once it is in operation, there really is not much more work having a corporation than filing a separate Schedule C form when you do your personal taxes.

In fixing up a non-residential property, some improvements can be deducted the year you spend the money, and other items will have to be depreciated over a number of years – which, in theory, is supposed to reflect the life of the improvement.

To help you keep track of all this, there are dozens of accounting software programs for sale. A system such as Quicken, for example, will let you easily keep track of building, art, and personal income and expenses. It is vital to know how much is being spent on utilities, for example, in order to learn if you are heating up the outside and that is why your expenses have skyrocketed. You will also get a better sense of your rental income by using this software program, and know if you should be pushing for some increases in rents the next time a studio becomes vacant. You will still use an accountant to do the annual tax returns, but you can quickly supply the data for those returns from your computer.

Leasing Part of the Space to Others. If you take over a large building, you will probably need to sublease part of it to offset your monthly expenses. In fact, this is by far the most effective way to make a purchase happen. You must become familiar with commercial leases if you are going to be renting spaces. Even if you don't lease out to others and rent a studio for your own use, you should become familiar with leases. Commercial leases are never standard. Don't ever be afraid to change a pre-printed, 'boilerplate' lease.

Leases. A commercial lease is a carefully written, legal document. If all goes well, it is never looked at after it is signed. But when a problem arises, then how well it has been written can become vital.

You can pick up boilerplate commercial leases from many sources. A sample commercial lease is enclosed at the end of this manual. Use it, amend it, and customize it as you wish; or just keep it to compare to other leases you might want to use.

Whether you are renting yourself, or renting space to others, it is important to understand the components of a commercial lease. Most contain the following:

Lessor: That's the name of the owner of the property.

Lessee: That's the name of the tenant, usually indicating a legal address or state of residence. Always insist on a personal name and not the name of a 'company.' You can add a company name (as well as other individual names if more than one person is sharing the studio), but unless you have a personal name on the lease, legally getting a judgment for past due rent may become impossible, because it's easy for a company to go out of business.

Date of Lease Agreement. Not the date of the term, but the date the lease is being prepared or signed.

Description, Term and Option to Renew. Often I make leases for one year, with an option to renew for an additional year with a 5% increase in rent.

You need to put in the address and unit number of the studio as well as the square footage. I also give a conservative size estimate, state that it is "approximate" with (+/-) after the footage amount.

One time a tenant rented a very large studio from me, moved in, and a few weeks later complained that the size had been inflated in the written lease and she wanted to pay less than the agreed-upon rent. She had measured each room and had come up with 500 square feet less than the lease stated. I measured, in her presence, the total length multiplied by the total width, and came up with more than the 3,500 square feet indicated in her lease. She had failed to take into account the thickness of all her interior walls.

In fact, many commercial leases for office space, for example, do 'inflate' the square footage and add 15% to the net square footage and charge, on a per foot basis, for this inflated amount. The 15% is supposed to account for the tenant's share of public hallways, bathrooms and lobbies, as well as for the thickness of the exterior walls.

I usually put in an option for the tenant to renew the lease for an additional year at a pre-set rental increase (usually 3-5%) with written notice ninety days before the lease term ends. Again, in practical terms, I rarely have an artist give me this notice. Sometimes, if I want tenants to be locked in for another year, I will send extension forms to sign and return to me. Most often, however, I add the increase, and legally the artists just remain as month-to-month tenants. They are taking a chance that I won't raise rates whenever I want, and of course, they have the option to tell me they are moving, after giving me thirty days' notice (which I don't always get unless I know informally what is happening). This doesn't worry me. because there is a strong market for good art space.

Representations of Landlord. Basically this says that the landlord has the right to rent the space.

Base Annual Rent. Write out the exact rent, multiplied by twelve months. If you are agreeing to less than a year, then change it to the base monthly rent. It's called a base because, in addition to the rent, there may be other payments for utilities, maintenance, or other services.

Use and Purpose. Spell out what the studio will be used for. Don't allow anything that you don't want, or will increase your insurance rates, or is not legal with local and state agencies. Keep it simple; I usually say the use will be for an "art studio, office, warehouse" to reflect my occupancy permit; otherwise I simply put "art studio."

For certain studios in one building, I also put in a clause that says that it may be permitted for artists to live in their studios as an accessory use, and that I, as landlord, give permission for the tenant to do so as long as it is accepted by governmental authorities. In other words, I don't want to be the one to say that the tenant has the right to live there, only for the tenant to then come after me if it is not all right or if the studio needs improvements to meet the code. In almost all communities where this might be accepted, I think it likely that there would be a mess as to what to do to satisfy the code, and I don't want to spend my time in that deep 'well.'

Assignment and Subletting. Don't allow someone to sublease unless you approve the new tenant and the use for the space. Also, if the tenant brings in 'partners,' that is like subletting; additional people in a space cause more expenses for the landlord. You should know about it up front. My rent is usually a bit higher if two people are sharing a studio rather than its being used by just one person.

Delivery of Possession. When will the space be ready? I usually put in that the space will be in an "as is" condition, so I don't set myself up for someone's getting in and immediately complaining about something.

Maintenance and Repairs. Landlords are usually responsible for the utility systems, roof, exterior walls and public areas. Tenants are usually responsible for their interior space. You can add a charge for snow removal or a fee for having a maintenance person clean the public areas; if you do, you should mention the amount where rent is stated or add a paragraph on "additional rent."

Utilities and Trash. Decide carefully who will pay what. When I am the landlord, I want to avoid paying for my tenants' utilities. If there are separate meters so tenants can pay for their electricity, that's best. Otherwise, I have to pay for heat and for electricity, but I limit it to existing lights. I state that tenants who are using air conditioners, machinery, kiln, heaters, and other equipment must pay for this additional use, such use to be estimated. That way, I can try to bill them if they run up my bills. If you allow tenants to have unlimited electricity for air conditioners, for example, your monthly electric bill might be as much as their rent.

Tenants always pay for telephone as well as cable service. It's hard to have tenants pay for heat if there is a central heating system or only a single meter for several studios. In one building where I control the heat with a set 24-hour system, while the tenants can only control their fans blowing out the heat, it doesn't matter. In my mill where studios have individual heaters on one gas line, I have a clause that states that tenants shall have a set amount of dollars for heat. If it goes over, they have to pay. I also state that tenants must make efforts to turn down thermostats when not in the premises. I might say that their use will be limited to 40 hours per week, or they pay extra for heat. The point is to have something in the lease that pretty much says that they should be as responsible as if they were paying the bills themselves, and if they are not, you have a right to bill them. It works to some effect to encourage tenants to turn down the thermostat when they go out.

Tenant's Fixtures and Equipment. Traditionally, if you screw something to the wall, it becomes the property of the landlord. So if shelves are built in, in theory the tenant cannot just rip them out and leave. In practice, artists will take anything they have installed and not pay attention to this. If they know in advance that they are going to make large improvements, I write it in that these will stay with the premises at the end of the occupancy - just as a reminder.

Often, I agree to reduce the rent or to give a month's free rent in exchange for some improvement that the artist has offered. It is a fifty-fifty chance that the improvement is worth having, in any case. In other instances, I have agreed to pay for the materials for some improvement. If it is a good job, the labor put in by the tenant becomes a real asset. It is much easier to have a tenant to do the work than for me to do it or even oversee it. Equipment belongs to the tenant. The times I get involved with that, and it's often, is when a tenant abandons stuff in moving out. Then it's my burden to get it into the dumpster. (If you rent to others, you'd better get used to being abused this way.)

Alterations. This says that a tenant may not make alterations to the premises without first getting the landlord's consent. Further, it says that the tenant shall pay for any alterations. Obviously, if both parties discuss making improvements in the beginning, then that should be specifically stated.

Liability and Fire and Extended Coverage Insurance. The landlord agrees to have general liability insurance and to insure the property against fire and other hazards. In fairness, if tenants have put a lot of time and money into their space, and there is damage to a public area that disrupts their ability to get access to or to use their rented space, the landlord has an obligation to fix the damage. That's why an insurance policy is necessary, because if the damage is serious, you won't be able to afford the repairs without insurance. This can also come under a heading of " Waiver of Subrogation – Landlord and Tenant."

Damage and Destruction. This spells out that you, as landlord, will repair the damage, and tenant will be responsible for tenant's premises. Although we are dealing with poor artists, commercial leases are drawn up as if the tenant is IBM.

Condemnation: It is highly unlikely (and only necessary for long-term leases), but if for some reason the government condemns or takes your property under 'eminent domain,' this spells out what happens and who gets what money.

Security Deposit. In most cases, I take "last month's rent" as a security deposit. If you take a straight deposit, in theory you are supposed to keep it in an interest-bearing account and return the deposit with interest to the tenant at the end of the term. If you call it last month's rent you can accept it just like rent. Usually you don't have to return it with interest, but again, check with the laws in your state regarding commercial leases. Having last month's rent gives you some protection if a tenant doesn't pay you. In North Adams, I don't take deposits and don't seem to have a problem. It depends on where you are, how many tenants you are dealing with, and how much money is involved. If you ask for first and last month's rent, and they have trouble coming up with it, it tells you how likely you are to get future rent payments from them, in full and on time.

Default. This basically spells out that rent is due on the first, and that there is a ten-day grace period after which the tenant is in legal default if rent has not been paid. Also, if a tenant violates any other clause in the lease, he/she is in default. It further spells out the steps that have to be taken. Make sure you put down that tenant is responsible for all legal and collection fees. You may not get them, but it helps to keep up the pressure. Also, I always add a 5% late fee if the rent is not received by the tenth of the month. If you don't, you will never get rent on time.

Subordination. You may have to refinance and/or the bank might want information from the tenants, and this just says that they have to comply. Banks might want to get tenants to sign a form stating they are indeed paying rent, to make sure you are not making the whole thing up. They may also want to have the leases assigned to them so if anything happens to you, or they have to take over the building, they already have in place a document from each renter that says that rent should be sent directly to the bank. In practical terms, I've had to do this once for a new mortgage, but the bank never demanded me to keep the document current, so new tenants were never part of this.

Quiet Enjoyment. This is actually a standard clause that basically says that if a tenant pays the rent and does not violate the lease, he/she is entitled to use the studio. I always add a sentence that he/she will not prevent other tenants from enjoying their studios due to objectionable noise, odors or activities. Again, it just allows a little pressure to be put on if a tenant's activities get out of hand.

Tenant's Liability and Indemnification of Landlord. This is careful legal language, which spells out that the landlord is responsible for certain aspects of the building, and is not responsible for others or for third-party lawsuits.

I always verbally explain to tenants that I have insurance that covers the building, but for whatever my insurance carrier won't cover, they should have their own insurance if they are worried about their equipment and supplies. For example, if an artist upstairs spills a five-gallon bucket of paint and the paint goes through the floor and drips on a tenant's computer in the studio below, that tenant can sue the upstairs tenant but he/she cannot sue the landlord, since the landlord was not negligent.

Inspection. The landlord has the right to get into a tenant's premises to repair, maintain, inspect (if bank or insurance agents have to see), and to show to prospective tenants three months (or some other period) before the lease expires.

Waiver: Basically, it says that if you don't enforce a default of one of the terms in the lease, it means that the tenant does not have the right to continue to be in default.

Holding Over: After the annual term, the lease continues in force on a month- to-month basis.

Notices. The address where legal notices should be mailed.

Entire Understanding. This lease is it. There are no verbal agreements outside of the written lease.

Governing Law. What state's laws the lease will follow in case of a dispute.

Severability. If one part of the lease is held to be invalid, the other parts still are valid.

Both parties sign and date two copies, with each party keeping one signed copy.

There could be other, probably minor, headings. There are many commercial leases out there. Not all leases fit all cases or states, and not all artists will be renting out part of their space. Certainly, I cannot give legal advice. But since renting to others is so important when acquiring a very large space, I wanted artists to have an idea of what is contained in a commercial lease. Plus, even if you have to be a tenant right now, this understanding will help.

Writing Leases. By far the easiest way to deal with leases is to get one that you are comfortable with and enter it into your computer so that every time you get a new tenant, it will only take a few minutes to change the name, unit number, rent and dates. You can also customize aspects, if utility responsibility is different, or if there are any special conditions that you have agreed upon.

I have a standard cover letter that restates the term and monthly rent, and the amount the tenant has to pay (deposit, for example) before the lease is fully signed and accepted and before he/she can get the keys to move in. It also states to whom the rental check is payable and where to send it. Very often artists can't get through a long lease, and it helps to summarize it for them. (A sample letter to use is included at the back of this book.)

COMMON PROBLEMS WITH TENANTS

These issues are addressed because, if you have a large studio where a portion is rented to others, you are dependent upon that income to pay your own bills. You don't want to jeopardize your ownership because a renter is not living up to his/her signed promises. Keeping the potential problems in mind is a way to detect early signs of trouble and hopefully to correct the problem before it substantially affects you.

Not Paying Rent. Not paying the rent is the most common tenant related problem although certainly not the only one. As an artist, I can sympathize with the sad tale of the struggling artist. But as an artist who owns a property requiring mortgage, utility, insurance, tax, and other payments to be made each month, my own struggles outweigh the struggles of my tenants. I've found, over the years, that the more I bend and allow tenants to get behind in their rent payments with promises such as "grant money being delayed," the more I end up losing in the end. Somehow, the tougher I get, the more money sudddenly appears from the tenant. A one-month security deposit gives you a little maneuvering room (two months' rent deposit is better, but usually not possible to get from artists). Since it is customary to give a tenant ten days after the first of the month before he/she is in default, by the time you then contact the tenant and find out what's going on, get a promise of a payment 'in the mail,' wait a few more days or even a week or so, then contact your lawyer to start eviction proceedings, and then go through that process, easily a month or two has passed.

Keep in mind that there are things you cannot do. You cannot personally throw someone out. You cannot change the locks to prevent a tenant from getting into his or her space. You cannot threaten that person.

You need to bite your tongue and deal with it in a lawful manner.

Getting Past-Due Rent Paid. Get right on it and call the tenant or see him/her in person. If you go in person, have something to write with and take a copy of the monthly rent invoice. I always write down on my copy of the monthly invoice when I've received payment, and what amount, and when I last communicated with them about their past-due rent.

Techniques for collecting past-due rents vary, but most collection experts agree that you want the tenant to acknowledge the debt, and to say specifically how much he/she will pay and when he/she will get it to you. Don't settle for a vague promise. Then if the tenant doesn't keep his/her promise, you can go straight to the lawyer to evict the tenant without feeling guilty. If you do this by telephone, get the promise and then repeat it back to the tenant: "You are sending me —— dollars by FedEx on —— day and so I will receive it on —— day. If I don't receive it then, I will have to start legal action." Remember, you've heard all the sob stories before; you have your own bills to pay.

Moving Out. Most of my tenants stay for a very long time; I offer great space at the most economical rates around. They sign leases, usually for one year at a time. I've found that when artists need to move, perhaps because of job opportunities, they will move, regardless of a signed lease. So I don't put much faith into long-term leases with artists, unless they seem very stable and affluent. For this reason, have at least one month's security deposit. If you have attractive space, you should be able to fill it.

My official policy is that I will release a tenant legally from the lease if I can find a satisfactory replacement tenant. That way, there is some incentive for the existing tenant to help me find someone.

Disruptions. Artists don't normally think of others. So they will hold parties, invite friends, allow for deliveries when they are not around, varnish a work without proper ventilation, and so forth. What you will have is trash – cigarette butts and beer cans – all over the public space, messy toilets, doors left ajar for anyone to walk in, and odors to chase you out of your own space. And this is just a short list. Either personally or through an artists' 'building committee,' get on top of it right away. Keep in mind that all of the negatives balance out against the positives.

CHAPTER 5
Design & Planning

*Watch a few programs like "This Old House" on TV.
Then do the opposite.*

Now that you have assessed the condition of the property, and are prepared to take over the space, you need to deal with the 'big box.' A huge shoebox space, as nice as it feels initially, is easily filled up and becomes ineffective to work in if left as is. What happens if you move in right away is that artwork and equipment are placed leaning against or near walls, and soon the interior space becomes smaller and smaller. New walls are good for delineating work areas, and well-placed walls allow works of art to be hung and shelves or workstations to be set against them. One twelve-foot-wide wall partition gives twenty-four feet of wall space on both sides.

When you start to think about a huge space, don't get sentimental; be functional. Love the space after you've finished renovations, not before. Well-designed space will pay dividends down the line, not only in your own studio operation but also in the economic return on your investment.

Old properties seldom can be moved into without doing some immediate repairs to the mechanical systems. Try at least to get the electricity and lights on so you can spend the time inside necessary for the planning stage.

Best Use. The idea of how to design the partitioning of a huge space really gets down to two main issues – your personal studio needs (which might even be in contradiction to economic logic) and the 'best use' of the building. The design can make or break the soundness of the purchase. When I first purchased my Washington warehouse, I could have rented out entire floors and spent less money on renovation. However, after examining possibilities and factoring in how the mechanical systems and maintenance issues would be affected, it made sense to spend more on the renovation in order to capture a better return, and to be able to deal with future issues while in the meantime keeping it artistically interesting, If there isn't enough income to pay for the monthly expenses, you are in trouble. In a 34,000-square-foot building, just having two or three artists to share the cost of heat, common electricity, taxes, insurance, and repairs – to name just the obvious ones – would not have worked. This became readily apparent by calculating the amount I would get per square foot (divide the total amount of annual rental income by the total amount of square footage). The square foot rental would not have been enough income to cover expenses. To chop it into little cubicles would not have worked either. The renovation and maintenance expenses would have been higher without the rental market supporting it. Creating a variety of mostly large, but some small and some medium- sized studio spaces, offered the best solution.

In the equation was not only my desire for a strong economic return, but also my ability to market the spaces. There was no sense in marketing office space in the neighborhood the building was in, nor did I have connections to office users. On the other extreme, I didn't look forward to sharing my building with a few laborers unloading or loading boxes. Dead storage just didn't seem like a business I wanted to get into. I knew artists, I knew the studio demand, and I felt comfortable with that role - especially at that time.

Don't try to be something that you are not. If you aren't comfortable with your intended use, think about design alternatives. Good design really starts with a business approach - rather than an aesthetic approach - to real estate. The role of the architect or designer is to bring the potential return of the property to reality.

DESIGNING

Design Basics. You have a shoebox of a space but you need to divide it into logical sections for working. First, you need to analyze your creative operation. If you dance, then obviously you will need a large dance floor and that will be the main portion of your space. Functional areas will radiate from this space. For the visual artist, probably the largest space will be devoted to the actual production area. Smaller areas can be used to create smaller works, and for a woodshop, an office, and so forth.

Once you've written down an outline of your needs, including some of the spaces you dream of (for example, I always wanted a separate woodshop so dust wouldn't carry over into my drawings), it is time to try to put them into an architectural sketch.

First, you have to know your building. Unless you already have architectural plans (and you should ask the owner, because often they do exist), that will mean going with a long measuring tape, pencil and graph paper to measure and draw the dimensions of the exterior walls, then the interior walls, columns, drains, main electrical panels, heaters, and other obvious components.

Make the drawing a good size, but it doesn't have to be huge. You need enough space to draw in new partitions and equipment. Do one page for each floor.

Then take the sketch and make a copy or two. Go to Kinko's and enlarge it into a blueprint size. They have blueprint copiers for that purpose. This becomes your main working plan.

First Approach. Once you have your existing space on paper, think of it like a blank canvas, with the existing walls as the boundaries of the canvas. When you paint on a canvas, compositionally you first break the rectangle into a few basic shapes, then gradually break it into smaller and smaller components as you add details. Designing a space is much like painting. Try to figure in your basic spaces, see if they fit with existing entrances, hallways and access points, and go from there. If you have an idea of how many basic units you need to get a 'best use' return, add your unit as the biggest, and play with these basic building blocks. As in creating, the more you experiment, the more you will learn of the dead ends and of the successes.

After you have spent some time learning the various combinations of spaces, think about the economics. If you are renting out to others, can you rent out $1,500-per-month spaces? Can you rent out $700 studios? Or $300 studios? You will have a good sense of what the market will bear in your community. Remember, in most cases you will need to start conservatively and plan on gradually increasing rents over a period of a few years. Your design should be based on the most conservative estimate of the amount for which you realistically can rent studios, factoring in the construction costs, not forgetting to include the cost of maintaining vacant spaces until they get filled.

If you want to stick to large units but fear that there won't be a market for expensive spaces, you can design them large, but add an eight-foot-high partition to divide them into smaller units. That way, you can rent to two or more artists and yet they will still have mostly private space. The partitions can even be made to move, either by hanging them or building them 'L' shaped so they can stand by themselves. This gives flexibility to the proportion of the division. At some point in the future you can create passages, or these partitions can be removed altogether to allow the studio unit to be used by one tenant.

On Paper. At any graphics or art store, buy a roll of tracing paper. Put the tracing paper over the building sketch and start designing.

Draw in all the units and public areas. Within your own studio space, draw in new partitions and try out different configurations. Box in where your table saw will be, your drawing table, your desk, and so forth.

Mentally (or virtually) walk into your plans, and then walk around the newly designed studio. Continue to mentally 'create' and go through all your work processes. If you need to stretch more canvas, where will you go to find the roll you're storing? If you need to show a dealer one of your works, where is she/he going to sit, and where are you going to lean the paintings or wheel out the sculptures?

Then try another design, take the evening off, and try again the next day. A good space design does not come instantly. Go through your entire list and make sure you have considered all of your operations.

If you are dividing up the building in order to rent out some spaces to other artists, start with your space first. Otherwise, you will lock yourself out of the best space. After all, you are doing the work, taking the risk, and have control. Treat yourself first and then deal with other spaces. Of course, you might have to retreat somewhat in order to satisfy building codes. For example, everyone needs at least two means of egress, so access to exits comes first.

Decide on what types of tenants you want, how much they can afford, and what size spaces you need to create. It will soon become a puzzle, because you also need to figure in access to bathrooms, sinks, windows, heaters, exits, and loading docks or other public areas.

Undoubtedly, you will go through the entire roll of tracing paper before you are satisfied with a plan. The last one you will draw more carefully and accurately.

By the way, if you need plans for the building department, these will do – especially if you enlarge your drawings and copy them into blueprints; they do not have to be as refined as those professional architects would submit. Each drawing will represent one floor; each drawing can also represent either electrical systems or plumbing or new partitions. If you are not doing too much, you can probably combine all the mechanical improvements onto one drawing. You do not need to show all existing systems, although new partitions, for example, need to be delineated from existing walls. The building department is basically interested in knowing what new stuff you are adding to the property. Go to a printer that can transfer your pencil drawings made blueprints.

One word about submitting architectural plans to building departments in your area. Some will insist that there be a certified architect or engineer. Most won't care, as long as licensed contractors are doing the work. In any case, don't be easily blown away by one governmental official who says that what you have submitted is not good. While they will encourage you to pay someone who is in the business, ask specific questions about what they want. In my experience, you can do it just fine and not pay someone else, mostly by standing in line and making small talk with code inspectors.

Obviously, if your project is ambitious and complex, then you will need professional help.

On Computer. There are various computer programs, some creating 3-D mock-ups from your measurements. If you are good at that, great, but I can sketch a design in about two minutes. There is no need to get involved with computers unless you are used to the program or want to do it for fun.

One advantage is that your computer-printed plans might be more professional looking and thus more acceptable to the building department.

Another advantage a computer-generated image has is the capacity to be e-mailed to prospective tenants, as well as to show the space as a three-dimensional design. This helps prospects visualize their potential space. If you have a lot of units to rent and think it would help, then do it. But I would not spend money hiring someone else. Do it yourself.

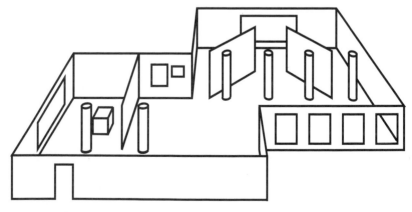

A 3-D design plan from a computer.

On the Floor. Use some tape, if the floor is clean enough. Otherwise, use two-by-four studs, or anything long and skinny, and place the lengths on the floor according to your layout. For the first time you can physically walk through your studio and see if everything makes sense. Sometimes you find that a space is not nearly big enough once you are standing in it; in this case, simply move your length of lumber until it feels right.

Another tip is that this is the best method to build your walls in the right place. Carpenters can just build where you place the wood, and not try to interpret architectural plans and transfer these measurements to your actual space. I've found that this also works wonders with plumbers and others who might have to do some rough-in work before the walls are even built.

Finally, no one will visualize the space the way you can. You've spent a lot more time with the design than anyone else. Especially if you are trying to rent space to others, they will only be able to visualize their potential space if you lay out the borders with lengths of tape or lumber.

With Models. At some point, you can even make a simple cardboard model (not for display but for your needs only). Take a length of cardboard only a few inches wide and fold it around the outside lines on one of your Kinko's copies. Then add some interior pieces for interior walls. You can simply draw doors and windows if you want. Cut up some wood blocks or Styrofoam pieces or whatever you can find, and place them to represent tables, desks, table saws, etc. Cut out a small figure made to the right proportion and put the figure inside your model. Study it and use it to make changes.

Partitions. I discuss partitions in the sections on construction and materials and give some ideas and tricks. I am adding them under design as well, because I have found that, since you are dealing with existing space, it is quite easy to construct some partitions early on and see if the design works. Whether you are using metal studs or two-by-four lumber, two people can build, flat on the floor, a ten-foot by sixteen-foot wall in about an hour. By standing up the wall, you will see the most dramatic part of your design come alive.

In constructing many spaces, I use this technique, then look carefully and see if I want to shorten the width, change the placement, or make some other adjustment. If I'm happy with it, then the partition is nailed or screwed into place. Having the basic partitions up also helps the electricians and plumbers do their rough-in work.

Not to put down virtual computer design, especially in this day and age, but actually building a few main partitions together with other two-by-fours nailed lightly to the floor, indicating the other planned walls, allows a full walk-through that will give you an idea of the final product, better than any other method.

If the construction of the walls of a rental studio is the first thing you do, it will be the most rewarding when you show the space to a prospective tenant.

Walls are quick and easy to build and can be moved around before sheet-rocking.

Architects. What can I say? If you have friends you respect who are architects, try to get their help for very little. If your project is large and complex, you will need help. I know it is a bias, but most architects are in love with their own details without proper regard to practicalities or to costs. Usually I'm the best architect, especially for the price! Admittedly, it's also because I now have quite a bit of experience. As artists, we have the creativity that others are looking for when they hire an architect. If you don't feel confident the first time you remodel, you might when you do your second studio.

The best experience I had working with an architect occurred when I asked for a basic design sketch and then midway through the construction, he came to the building and gave me, on the spot, some suggestions for a few tricks that would jazz things up a bit. But basic decisions about building materials and methods were made by getting prices of materials from the lumberyards and by talking to the contractors. I much prefer this method than having detailed blueprints to follow.

Of course you can demand from your contractors that they follow what the architectural blueprint calls for. They will say that anything can be done but it will end up costing you double. I always 'go with the flow' to lower expenses. Rarely do blueprints anticipate all the problems you will run into during remodeling projects. You will also have a lower architectural bill because you are not paying that person to draw up mechanical plans as well.

If you have full-blown architectural plans and can't change them on the spot during construction without consulting with the architect, you might as well add 25% to your total costs right from the beginning. The point is, you must be in charge of the project and feel confident in your decisions.

Design features can be added along the way. These ideas might be a color for a wall, or making a fake column, or adding an angle to a corner. Once I spent about $200 building a round wall (there's a special way to do it with sheetrock) at the suggestion of an architect who walked in and proposed it instead of a flat wall as a partition between two rooms. A few years later, I probably got $20,000 extra for my house because of that design feature.

People will walk in and get blown away by a few design highlights and then not even remember what kind of existing heating system there is, or other more substantial matters. Every space has potential, and if you can't bring it out there's nothing wrong with getting help.

I am just adding the caution that a full set of plans does not ordinarily save you money in construction, contrary to what many architects will tell you. In all probability, you will be working with an existing space. You are not doing new construction from the ground up.

The exception to this is if you are doing structural work; then you had better get a qualified engineer to tell you what sizes of beams and posts to use. In most cases, you won't be dealing with that in an existing space.

Additionally, this manual will continue to stress that you can take a dollar and stretch it very far. If you spend a modest $2,000 on an architect, you have $2,000 less to use for the renovation. That much money can buy you all the studs and sheetrock you will need to build hundreds of feet of walls. However, if your project is large, and the $2,000 represents only 2% of the total construction costs, then that might be acceptable. If it represents 10% of your costs, then I would reconsider.

Finally, just a reminder that plans do not have to be submitted to the building department in order to have a lot of mechanical work performed. Plumbing and electrical contractors can pull their own permits for their work. Adding hallways or rental units does require plans, but some buildings can be divided without extensive construction. Do whatever the building calls for, but don't go overboard.

Go with the Flow. If you've taken over a former manufacturing space, it probably has offices and storage rooms. Don't try to start from scratch; it will only cost you money for very little gain. Try to incorporate the existing rooms into your plans.

Take your rough plans and talk to the contractors. They will give you suggestions about what not to do from their point of view. Ask them if your plans are increasing their work and therefore your costs.

Throughout a renovation, you will have to make instant, on-the-spot decisions. Sometimes I bite the bullet and insist on something that will cost more, but usually I try to bend to get the contractors out of there. Their time is costing me money.

Preservation. Keep the interesting parts of your space: mill floors, old brick walls, antiquated bathroom fixtures (such as gang sinks and heavy, old faucets) exhaust fans, old windows, ramps, and metal floor plates and other artifacts from the building's previous life. Not only are these 'retro' and in fashion, but they maintain a certain honesty about your renovation.

In MASS MoCA, a beautiful new museum complex in a former textile mill, bathroom walls that had once been painted green and pink were left alone, even though they are now part of the main gallery spaces.

You will be glad you kept them when you point out these features to visitors. It may help you get future grants, because being sensitive to the past is credited highly in applications for funding.

Copy Successful Spaces. Design magazines, architectural loft books, new office buildings, and anything that you stumble across that captures your eye – all are sources for ideas that you can use. Don't worry about how much someone else paid, because there are always cheaper ways to do it.

If you are in love with Japanese gardens, put a few rocks and river stones right in a public, interior space. Don't have any rocks? Make them out of Styrofoam and paint them. Do you like marble columns? Get a Sonotube (a cardboard tube used to pour concrete columns) from the lumberyard and paint it to look like marble. Faux is in and anyone can do it. There are more ideas later in the manual, but the main idea is that others have spent thousands of dollars for designers and architects. You are dealing with an old, industrial property. You can get away with a great deal without spending a lot, and still end up with an awesome space.

This Old House. As you deal with the design for the transformation of commercial or industrial space into arts use, you might fall in love with many building components – the exposed brick and beams, heavy columns, floors that can take heavy loads, large industrial windows. That's fine if you can be satisfied with the way they are. You might want to bring these features out.

That's also fine if you can do it in a simple way. However, there are some people who overdo it. This tendency can be seen in people who buy an old house and methodically remove old paint to expose the original wood in the railings, window and door trim, floors, etc. This can be beautiful in a house. Watch a few programs like "This Old House" on TV. Then do the opposite. Don't get carried away or be too fussy when you have 20,000 square feet of space to transform.

People walk into our loft all the time and say, "Wow!" It really is dramatic space. But if I were to point out all the details, you would see imperfections that would not be acceptable in any normal house. Walls that have bumps and cracks and drywall compound ridges, for example. Were walls put up and finished by bad workers? No, when you are hustling 200 feet of walls, you can't always bother to go over it with a fine-tooth comb. It doesn't matter. If it did, you would be spending $50 per square foot just in renovations, rather than $2. In addition, just to begin with, we were dealing with floors that sloped more than six inches for every ten feet in places, as well as ceilings and floors that had dozens of holes drilled for pipes and some holes covered with metal plates. With all these existing imperfections, it didn't make sense to make the place look as if it was built yesterday. I've seen mills where, by the time they have finished installing new windows, new walls, new stairs, drop ceilings, and new carpet, the only indication of it having been a mill is the exposed exterior brick. It is not necessary to cover up everything.

It is what it is. If you need a museum-type result, then use the best architects and contractors money can buy. But even museums (like MASS MoCA) will want to leave most of the structure alone. If you are going to follow the advice in this manual, then don't get bogged down and lose money or time over details that will never be noticed in the end. Of course, if a few details bother you at the end of the renovation, you can always go back and deal with them individually.

CHAPTER 6
Construction

*Be very careful about what you toss out when you first
take procession of a studio building. Existing systems
usually are there for a reason.*

Construction time becomes the real acid test for
turning a large shoebox into a functional, working studio.
Up to now, you've dealt with quick problems.
Construction, fixing up the studio, renovation or
remodeling – whatever you want to call it – can go on for a
very long time.

It's like having a baby; there's so much excitement
and attention paid to the pregnancy, naming and delivery.
But then you bring your baby home and suddenly you
realize that you have little preparation on how to raise your
son or daughter for the next eighteen-plus years. Until the
construction stage, all the excitement was about
negotiating, funding, designing and taking procession.
Now you have to deal with the physical structure.

As you read about various construction items, you
will notice that I have two tendencies. One is to not spend
money unless necessary, and to find a cheaper way of
doing things. Most of an existing building can be left alone
and done later.

The other tendency, however, is to spend a bit more
to save a lot more in the future. If, for example, you are
having the electrician coming to do some work, for a bit
more you can add extra electrical outlets, lights, or add
some other feature that would cost you a lot more if you
had to do it as a separate item. Be careful not to get
carried away. Another example is to spend more in order
to increase rental income.

One word of caution: I've mentioned in several
places that artists might be able to do their own work to
save on hiring contractors. In some communities, it is
acceptable to do plumbing and electrical work yourself,
except where connections are made to main lines. In other

communities, only a licensed contractor can make changes to any electrical or plumbing fixture, wire, pipe or connection. In truth, artists will do a lot of the work regardless of building codes, but they should be aware that they do so at their own risk. The building department might object or their work might cause damage or injury. Some areas might be safer than others; running the electrical conduit, which is just the housing for the wires, probably would be accepted in most places if it is acceptable to the electrical contractor who has to be responsible for the finished work. So, when in doubt, check with the building department and with your contractor.

Re-Do the "Before Settlement" Steps. You've gone through a lot of investigation before you settled and took procession of the studio property; now you have to do it again. Before you write any checks for work to be performed, you want to know what are the absolutely least expensive and most logical things to do.

Also, make sure that insurance and utility accounts are all active and in your name.

Priorities. Some repairs might have to be made immediately. Water damage is usually the most important because it never gets better, only worse. If you need heat to get through the winter, you have to determine how much heat to at least prevent pipes from freezing, unless you drain all the water lines with air pressure. You need to make sure the property is secure to avoid a break in. You need light and electricity to operate tools.

Then you need to examine your plans carefully. You need to determine whether new electrical wires or plumbing pipes have to be installed inside of walls before the walls are finished with sheetrock. Make a list of what has to be done and then put it into a schedule.

Sectionalize. Don't take on more than you can handle. Do one section first, perhaps, in a way that makes sense. Maybe the second floor is not an immediate need and you can deal with that another year. Perhaps you need to do the tenants' spaces first in order to get them rented, and then come back to do your own studio. It might delay things somewhat, but it will probably also be a big cost saver. You will make mistakes, but you will make fewer mistakes the second time around. Get your feet wet before you dive in. That doesn't mean that certain items shouldn't be addressed. If you need to rough-in new electrical lines, at least get power to the spaces not being addressed, so that you don't have to come back into finished spaces.

One imperative is that rental space should be completed in order to get income. If you have tenants lined up, get their spaces ready. Also, even if you don't have tenants, at least do one space so that you have something to show prospective tenants. Remember, they will not have the imagination to visualize the studio space as you do. Build the walls and put in the door, and you will have a physical, private space to rent.

It is hard to advise without knowing the specifics, and of course it is a conflict when most artist/owners want to get into their studios and get back to work, but much of this is a one-time proposition.

If the project is very large, then you will have no choice but to do it in stages. In order to keep up with your studio work, once the initial construction has been completed, try to schedule additional construction during a set period each year, for example, or limit the hours so you can do your own work. When I did the 130,000-square-foot mill, of course I did not have the money to do it all; I concentrated on some sections and used as much as I could of the other sections, even though they were in rough shape. Each year we did additional areas, within a budget and in such a way that my studio work could continue. Gradually, the time I needed to devote to construction decreased.

Be careful about spreading yourself too thin. You can save money by doing some of the easy stuff such as cleaning and drilling holes in studs, rather than have expensive workers do it, but this will take energy away from other things you need to handle. It might pay for you to supervise only, and hire some minimum-wage workers to do that work as well.

Sears Shop Vac: an indispensable piece of equipment for construction and for studio use. Get one for each floor. Great for emergency floods as well.

Cleaning. Wear a mask and sweep out the entire place. Do it before you even think about what some of the dirt might contain. Keep furniture and shelving, but get a dumpster and throw everything loose into it. Get rid of it. (It's best if you can get the seller to agree to transfer the property to you 'broom-clean.' That way you don't have to get into any issues about what is going into the dumpster.)

If you don't discard, you will be moving materials ('trash' as you will later find out) from one area to another. I cannot deny that I am a pack rat because I use so many types of materials in my art, but I have also found that there are limits. When you have moved heavy stuff that you are saving for the tenth time in a ten-year period, you will finally learn that you really never needed it to begin with.

The only exception to this would be to save a few artifacts, if any exist, that would indicate the history of the building. They might be fun to have for some future date when the entire space has been transformed into an art or creative studio.

You are about to use the space for making art. For much of the creative work, you probably require a clean space, especially for paper works. The continuous headache, after you have moved in and spent time working in the studio, is dust coming from the ceiling. Most industrial buildings contain exposed beams, ducts and pipes. Over decades, dirt piles up; when there is a vibration, it will fall down onto your nice white paper. It is much easier to deal with immediately, before one item has been moved in.

There are various methods, none of them quick. You can climb a ladder with a strong vacuum cleaner and go over every square inch of surface. One time I hired a contractor with a gigantic compressor on a trailer, and with a fire hose and all the windows opened, we blew off as much of the accumulated dust as we could. The problem was that the joists and braces were only 13 inches apart, and the dust over a century had settled and become packed down, and despite our efforts, most of it still remained.

The other solution is to clean off the ducts and pipes and cover the ceiling itself with sheetrock or other insulation materials. You may not be able to do it all, but some attempt at cleaning or sealing by paint spraying these surfaces will be worthwhile.

Building Permits and Inspections. Every region will have different procedures for you to follow. In many cases, the electrical and plumbing contractors can get their own permits. Generally, once you know what improvements you will be making, you need to submit plans and to get them approved. The building department will give you a "building permit." You can then proceed with the work. Typically, electrical and plumbing work has to be inspected while the walls are not covered with sheetrock. That way the inspector can actually see all the connections. Once the rough-in is approved, you can go ahead and cover the partitions with sheetrock. When the construction is all completed, the various inspectors (in smaller communities, one inspector might cover different aspects) will go over the work and hopefully approve it. At that time, you can go back to the building department and get your "occupancy permit," which is your right to occupy the premises.

Obviously, the inspectors are experienced and have seen it all. At the same time, try not to advertise everything you are doing. Stick to the work submitted in your plans and deal with the basic elements in the raw space. You can always go back to do cosmetics.

Suppliers. Get to know your suppliers. It is so convenient when you can simply call up and get something delivered without having to go to the store.

Always ask for a contractor's account and price. I can't tell you how much money people waste because they don't know that all you have to do is ask, and almost all suppliers will give you a discount. Sometimes it saves 10% or more, which can really add up. Paint stores, hardware stores, lumberyards – always ask. Tell them you are acting as the contractor for the building. They can only say no.

I hate to give business to one chain, but Home Depot is so large that there must be one close to you. They will also deliver. Although I deal with local stores, in one case, it paid for me to put several orders together and have Home Depot truck it to me. They can really under-price almost everyone. When there is a big difference in cost, you can't ignore them.

Harbor Freight (800-423-2567 or harborfreight.com) and Northern Tool and Equipment Co. (800-556-7885 or northerntool.com) are two tool supply catalogs to check out. You can get everything from lifts to sprayers to market umbrellas. Once they have your address, catalogs will be arriving continually. Get the lower-priced tools when you have a choice. The chances are that the tool will disappear before it breaks. It's also nice to have more than one of all the essential tools around a large building.

Safety. The construction period is actually a dangerous time. As will be mentioned later, there are issues that should be addressed to make your building and studio a safer environment. Most people don't get into this until they have moved in and are operational. However, during construction, you may have many people putting your property at risk by smoking or using torches and welders. You will not know the property well (for all you know, the floors could be saturated with oil), and generally there are more loose ends than you can keep up with.

Prior to construction is the time to do a careful walk- through, purchase fire extinguishers and a medical kit, and make anyone working in the building aware of fire and safety issues. Also, make sure your insurance policy protects you during this period.

Roof. Keep water out. That's one of the basic rules. Most problems in buildings will remain stable. Water coming in will only get worse, never better. Deal with it quickly.

Commercial roofs come in various types: flat roofs that have a slight pitch might be built-up asphalt or rubber. Roofs that have more of a pitch might also be metal, slate, shingle, or asphalt tile. Often, large buildings with appendages will have more than one type of roof.

I've inspected large mills, including one of 180,000 square feet that I thought was a bargain, until I saw that the entire 40,000-square-foot roof had to be replaced. Suddenly, adding $120,000 to the purchase price made it less attractive. Another building had a waterfall pouring in. But 95% of the water came from a small flat roof that the owners didn't want to fix. I was able to repair the roof for a reasonable cost and the building ended up being a bargain. In a nearby town, a mill that would have made a wonderful artists' building is now being demolished. Why? Because the town (which took control of it when the previous owners left town with taxes unpaid) wouldn't pay $300 (not a misprint - just a few hundred dollars) to patch the roof, and three years of water destroyed the entire structure. That was a one-million-dollar mistake the town made.

If you can find a building with ten more years of life in the existing roof, the economics might make sense. Roofs can be patched. A new roof can last anywhere from twenty to forty years, although most roofers will tell you that forty years might be pushing it.

If you have a clean, rectangular roof with a minimum of vents interrupting the surface, a new roof might cost you about $2.00 a square foot for very large areas -usually more, however. I've mentioned this before, but talk to several roof contractors. They will also recommend the roofing system appropriate for your building and to the region. What suppliers have in stock will always cost less than materials needing special shipping. Roofers' estimates will vary greatly. If you want a good idea of costs, call up the supplier and find out what the materials will run; then double that amount to account for labor. It could run you less, but certainly not more.

For one roof, I had polyurethane foam sprayed onto the old roof, which was still in fair condition. This gave me a new roof (it is a standard roofing system) and at the same time it insulated the roof without my having to insulate from the inside, which would have covered up a beautiful, exposed loft ceiling.

If you need to replace a roof, and there is a good pitch, I would recommend a metal roof; aesthetically, it looks great on barns and all kinds of buildings because you can purchase the metal in a wide range of colors.

If you have a flat roof, rubber is probably the most effective way to go. Basically, rolls of rubber roofing are overlapped, and the seams are sealed together with heat. Using 'torch-down' rubber roofing, the entire surface is heated up with a torch to melt the 'glue' on the underside.

Old buildings will probably have built-up asphalt roofs. For medium-size or smaller roofs, you can purchase "double coverage" rolls and mop on a roof cement to hold the roofing material down. This is the cheapest way to repair or replace small roof sections, and you don't have to be an expert to put it on. Obviously it helps to have it done by a professional roofer, but if you get stuck, it can be done by others – a carpenter, maintenance person, or anyone who has had some experience.

There are lots of sealers and products to use for leaks. Some can even be applied when the surface is wet. You should check the roof while it is raining and watch how the water runs off the roof. If water is getting into the building, it is starting somewhere and entering. Sometimes it gets under the roof in one place, but then runs quite a distance before it drops down into the interior space. Look at the flashing. Most water leaks occur at the flashing, near the edges or where there are vents or other interruptions on the roof.

Most roof problems are a result of people walking on them. Keep people off your roof, but if you need to walk on it, do so carefully.

Structural. This covers many types of potential problems. Most buildings have to support upper floors and/or a roof. Buildings can have columns (metal or wood) to carry ceiling joists or roof joists. This entire skeleton needs to be in good, solid condition. Water, moisture, dryness, insects and physical abuse can all damage these elements. Other structural elements are exterior walls and interior structural walls. Walls built to carry weight above can be made of wood or metal studs, brick or block. Although you wouldn't think of them as being fragile, these elements can still get damaged.

Freezing water, for example, can break brick apart. The mortar used between bricks might have deteriorated. Pointing up is a method of cleaning out the loose mortar and with a narrow trowel blade, pushing new mortar into the cavities. It takes time, but anyone can do it.

Where brick walls are no longer solid and vertical, sections may have to be taken down and rebuilt. I took possession of a church where there were many sections with brick falling apart. One reason I got the building so cheaply was that I told the owner that the building probably would not make it through another winter, and that he would then have a huge expense demolishing the property. A previous potential purchaser had gotten an estimate of about $30,000 to make these repairs. I hired a mason, by the hour, and he did all the work for about $4,000. At the same time, my accepted offer was about $30,000 less then the previous offer and a bargain for sure, when I got the 9,000-square-foot church for $47,000. In another case, a barn roof was sloping. The beam was pushed up with an inexpensive hydraulic jack until it was straight, and a block was put under the column base. The whole job took about two hours. The point is that, often, large problems can be itemized and dealt with for reasonable costs.

Sometimes one section of a building will have structural problems. As an alternative, consider taking that section out. For example, in renovating the museum galleries, the architects for MASS MoCA decided not to rebuild an entire floor section that was rotten; they simply took it away, thereby creating a spectacular two-story space. While you lose floor footage, you create something very special. I've seen other buildings where similar decisions have been made.

Insulation. Usually you don't get the economic benefits of insulation that you would have insulating a residencial property. In a house, the idea is that if you turn down your thermostat, the heat will stay inside and the house will only slowly get cooler. In most industrial buildings, you probably won't have much insulation, and so when the heater is turned off, the space cools quickly. In a house, you insulate walls and then cover with wallboard (sheetrock). With industrial buildings where you have exposed brick, for example, it is difficult to insulate without also doing additional wall work.

Additionally, the sizes are so large that it would be an expensive job to insulate, and the payback period would be many years.

This is not to say that you don't take the obvious measures. If you have large windows with single-pane window glass, a second layer of glass, plexiglas or plastic during winter months will not only make a difference in your heating bill, but also make the studio more comfortable by preventing cold drafts. You might have some walls where insulation can make a difference, not just in heating or cooling, but also for sound deadening. Rolls of fiberglass insulation can be stapled between studs. Make sure you get the right width, and wear gloves. Some people have an allergic reaction to the fiberglass fibers.

You should seal up any openings where cold air is coming in. This might mean stuffing or foaming insulation around pipes and windows and under doors and other openings.

I usually seal off sections where heat may not be needed as much, in order to concentrate the heat where I am working. Heating storage areas, for example, is usually a waste.

For summer, I insulated a ceiling by applying foam on the exterior of the roof; this prevented a lot of heat from coming in. By applying foam, I got a new roof at the same time and killed two birds with one stone. Before then, my gallery dealer, who had a top-floor gallery, once had a plastic sculpture melt. Of course, part of the problem was that all the windows were closed when the gallery was not in use, and the space heated up like an attic without a ventilation exhaust fan. Insulation inside might cover up the exposed brick or wood that gives your space interest. You will have to choose between keeping the aesthetic and reducing costs.

Summer is the time when you think about keeping the heat out and perhaps cooling the place. I know few studios where artists can afford more than one air-conditioning unit in a critical area (bedroom or office), but ventilation fans, ceiling fans and cross-ventilation from open windows go a long way.

A large studio with high ceilings, on the top floor of a four-story warehouse building. This artist stapled fiberglass insulation between the ceiling joists, with the foil facing the studio. Whether you like the metallic look or not, it enables the studio to remain cool with just one window unit. (Artist Stevens Carter)

Heating and Air Conditioning. Unless you are lucky and live in a place where heat is not necessary, heat will be one of your biggest expenses if you have a big studio. I don't know if I could have carried out all my art activities in the mill I currently own, if it had a central heating system. Not being able to afford to heat 130,000 square feet, I drain the pipes in sections of the mill and leave them cold. In those sections, I can still use them in winter months by turning on the heaters shortly before I intend to work. The main inconvenience is that I have to walk farther to a heated space to get water. But economically I couldn't afford to heat this much space only for my own use. The mill used to have almost 800 employees working in it; now it has a few dozen artists. You must adjust the economics to make sense of large spaces. (My tenants have better heat because they only rent 1,000- to 3,000-square-foot studios.) By contrast, in my Washington, DC, studio building, the former warehouse had a central boiler. By renting out 15 studios in addition to my own large space, I could pay for the heat and keep the entire building comfortable.

Instead of a large boiler system, the mill has mostly hanging (gas/propane) heaters that blow out hot air. It is the cheapest way of heating a space. You can hang one heater and it can take care of a space that is 5,000 square feet. Each unit costs about $800. (Check the Grainger catalog at www.grainger.com. They come in various sizes.) You need to double that amount to include installation. This system is usually found in garages and large warehouses, where evenly distributed heat is not crucial. For office space, it is much nicer to spend an additional amount for a system that feeds hot air into a duct. The ductwork can be run exposed, and it distributes the heat more evenly because you can install vents wherever they are needed.

Again, check with several distributors and contractors. Get prices and find out how much they are charging you for the heater. Ask how much they would charge if you supply the units. They could be marking up the same Grainger unit as much as 100%.

Air conditioning presents the same problems as

heating. You need to compare prices. Except for an occasional window unit, you probably won't be having to air condition large spaces, unless you live in a place like Houston, Texas, where artwork will rot away in no time unless humidity is controlled. Then you are spending more on cooling than others might spend on heating.

A gas space heater. Simple and effective, it can be located inside the studio space and needs no ductwork except for ventilation. It is similar to a gas oven; when the cylinders get heated, a powerful fan blows out the hot air. Photo by Caroline Bonnivier

If you can separately heat and separately meter tenants' spaces and let them pay for their own heat that will be great. Otherwise, you will have to include their heat as part of their rent. In the case of a central system, I have a locked control unit so that the heat comes on full-blast in the morning, and then in the late afternoon it goes into a night cycle. The building is still warm, even at night, but artists who want extra heat because they are 'living' in their studios or working late can always have extra electric heaters hooked up to their electric meters. The system also adjusts the heat according to outside temperatures. If I didn't have this system, and heated 24 hours a day at the same rate regardless of outside temperatures, my bill would be more than double. Check into this system when you talk to your heating contractor.

Be very careful about what you toss out when you first take procession of a studio building. Existing systems are usually there for a reason. I once was advised by an architect to change the heating systems, and I threw out several large radiators. It cost me a few thousand dollars to buy second-hand radiators to replace the ones I had tossed a month earlier. That's when I learned that, before you make changes, you'd better have lived through a winter season so you know the real needs.

Finally, contact the utility companies. I replaced an old boiler when the gas company offered me a 50% rebate. This was a $20,000 boiler, installed, which cost me $10,000. It also came with financing by the gas company. In addition, the purpose of the rebate was to conserve energy, and my heating bills went down almost 20%, easily paying the additional expense of the new boiler in just a couple of years.

Sprinkler Systems. I spend more time worrying about the sprinkler system than I do about fire. A sprinkler system is a series of pipes that cover the entire ceiling area of a building. The pipes have "sprinkler heads" that are located every few feet, so that water can put out a fire no matter where in the building it starts.

In a wet system, the pipes are always filled with water and under pressure. The idea is that a fire will melt the lead seal of a sprinkler head, and water will rush out and flood the area, hopefully putting out the fire. The system is like a stiff water hose.

In a dry system, the pipes are filled with air under pressure. When the lead melts, the air escapes. When the pressure suddenly drops, it flips a valve that sends water into the system. Within a minute or two, water fills all of the pipes and escapes at the opened sprinkler head(s).

The first problem with sprinkler systems is that you need a pretty good bonfire to melt lead that is placed at the ceiling. In an industrial building, the sprinkler heads can be ten to twelve feet high.

The second problem is that either you need to constantly heat the space for a wet system, which costs money, or in a dry system that can normally sustain the cold, be fearful that water will creep into the pipes and freeze (seals and valves often leak). If freezing causes the pipe to break, water will rush in as if it's a fire, and come out the opening, and then you have a flood on the floor, pipes filled with water in a unheated space, the fire engines at your front door, and, par for the course, this happens at three o'clock in the morning on a Sunday when the plumbers are least available. If the pipes aren't drained immediately before they freeze up, more problems will occur. When you have a lot of space, it's hard to control it all, and economically it is hard to keep all spaces heated during winter months.

Insurance companies and local building codes might require you to maintain the sprinkler system. Certainly it helps to prevent a serious fire from wiping you out.

In one building, however, no system was in place. I elected to install a smoke and heat detector system rather than a sprinkler system. My feeling was that I wanted to detect a fire long before it would grow into a bonfire. This system still qualified the building for lower insurance rates. Because of new building codes, this might no longer be acceptable.

If you end up with an existing sprinkler system, you will have a slight nagging feeling, especially during winter nights and deep freezes. Do not rush into sprinkler repairs until you understand the system and what really has to be done. Normally, a good plumbing contractor will be able to reset valves and replace heads or broken pipes. Once your system is activated, it's a real concern.

If you have a wet system, consider changing it to a dry system where freezing temperatures won't break the pipes and set off the system. You can also sign up for a maintenance agreement that will service your main control station.

We have heaters in the sprinkler stations, and through small windows the pressures and temperature can be checked regularly. Of course, you may want to install a backup system in case of power failure, compressor failure or some other malfunction.

You might also want to do an alarm test and fire drill. You will probably notice no one exiting the building. You then might point out to your tenants that this could be a dangerous assumption in case of a real fire.

Electrical. I know enough about electrical installation not to do it. Many artists I know seem to be good at it. If you can bend conduit pipe (the bender is just $30), you can save the $40 per hour (+/-) cost of labor having a licensed electrician do that aspect of the work.

In most cases, you are dealing with industrial spaces where little has to be hidden. Wires either go in a wall (when they are in walls you can use Romex wire) or they are outside the wall in a metal shield, either stiff conduit pipe where the actual wires are snaked through, or in metal clad, flexible cable that already has a metal skin (metal clad is commonly called BX, but BX doesn't have a ground wire and metal clad does).

If you make a list of what you want, that helps. Most important to saving money is to have the actual locations marked – on paper as well as on the walls – so that, when an electrician comes, you are not wasting his/her time. I've spent many an hour being the assistant. I'm around if there's a question, to give a hand and to sweep up afterwards. I don't want to pay high wages for cleanup type work.

Invariably, every time I have electrical work performed when I am away, something is not put in the correct place, something is not finished, necessitating a return trip, or something has been installed that I didn't want. You can write it down, you can diagram it, and you can even have an electrician visit prior to the work being done, but if you are not there, it will cost you more.

As I will mention later, think about the outlets you need; avoid having extension cords all over your floor. If you have a table saw, think about having an outlet right next to the saw so you won't trip over a cord while cutting lumber.

A major concern will be the places where you require heavy electrical use. Kilns and other heaters draw a lot of power. Find out if you have single-phase or three-phase electrical service, which might influence what type of equipment can be used.

In almost all cases, however, industrial spaces will have more electrical power than your art processes will require. If you are taking a shell of a building with few existing components, then I would suggest you run one main line and not try to put outlets every ten feet. Concentrate your electrical needs and design your space to avoid extra construction.

As in other trades, which contractor you hire can make a big difference. Always the best approach is to put your needs on paper, get several bids, then stick with the list and try not to have many additions. Also, ask in advance what an additional outlet, for example, would cost you. While not a hard and fast rule, generally when contractors give a bid on a job, they are padding it a bit to protect themselves. In addition, while you may be happy with the bid, undoubtedly there will be cost overruns because of changes and additions. Another approach to take, if you suspect that the job will be open-ended, is to accept one of the lower bids by deciding with whom you are comfortable, who has the lowest hourly rate, and who will personally be on the job (a smaller outfit). Find out what materials and associated costs are included in the bid. You might be able to shop around for the large items. Then hire them on a time and materials basis. You will have to oversee the work and make sure they are not getting distracted. If, on the other hand, you have finite plans and are very confident that you will not get sidetracked at all, then a bid may be the way to go, because the crew will come in and do the work fast.

If you feel that the bids are much too high, they probably are. Don't give up until you have exhausted the firms in your area. I've seen bids go down by half, so the savings can be significant.

If you are paying for new materials, make sure that your contractor is installing new materials. I've seen materials being installed which were pulled from other jobs. That may be fine, because conduit is conduit, but if you are getting used materials then the bill should be adjusted downward to reflect this.

Lighting. I have done some pretty fancy spaces for galleries and living lofts as well as for workspaces, and in all cases I have not hesitated to use the cheapest, basic electrical conduit and light holders I could find. The 'industrial' look is in, and it's better than wasting money on track systems.

There are three basic types of lighting systems I've used. The basic for work areas is fluorescent fixtures. While artists might not like this type of light, it's cheap and easy. I've always said that any art that looks good in studio light will look great under gallery light. I've also installed "daylight" fluorescent bulbs, but I can't say I've been impressed with the difference.

The second system uses standard bulb holders attached to the conduit. These cheap fixtures (probably two dollars or so each) allow a floodlight bulb to rotate and swivel, so they're perfect to use for gallery lights. I use bulbs that vary from 55 watts to 150-watt floods. You can buy these functional fixtures to hold one, two or three bulbs at each junction. Placed every ten feet or so, you can light up a space just like an art gallery.

The third system I use to get gallery light is a cheap, rectangular halogen light that you can pick up at any hardware store for eight to fifteen dollars. It is so bright that one light will do a large area. They tend to get hot, you have some rotation and swing adjustment (but not as much as the plain swivel fixtures above), but at that price they can't be beat.

Avoid the track systems. They look great, but it's overkill for industrial space. They cost a fortune. One time I did use track (naturally, on the advice of an architect) and years later I couldn't find compatible fixtures when I needed to add some.

Make sure fixtures are installed where they can be easily reached. I've seen too many lights installed over staircases necessitating the use of tall ladders simply to change a bulb. Allow for energy saving bulbs and fixtures in common, functional spaces where lights have to remain on twenty-four hours a day. There are various devices, from solar sensors to motion detectors to timers that can minimize energy costs.

There are ways to direct sunlight into dark areas. I sometimes add clear or translucent panels above doors so that light in a studio will also penetrate the windowless hallway, while maintaining the artist's privacy.

The cheapest lighting system in this case is the most effective and attractive for a loft. In working spaces, I use eight-foot fluorescent fixtures. Pictured above are bare flood lights in exposed holders and conduit. Notice nearby the exposed duct work and painted sprinkler systems. You worry as much about a flood from the sprinkler pipe or a head freezing and breaking as you do about a real fire.

Plumbing. Plumbing is getting easier these days. Copper pipes are easy to run. PVC is used for almost all drain and vent pipes, and you probably won't need anything fancy. In fact, shop around. Basic fiberglass utility sinks are inexpensive. You may want to go to a building supply store and find other items. Cheap showers come in one piece, and can be used to shower as well as to hose down silk screens or for other art processes (such as your 'loft' needs). You might want to consider a washer and dryer if you are going to live in the studio, because my guess is that laundromats might not be close by.

You might be tempted to do a lot of the work yourself and just use a licensed contractor where it gets complicated.

Be creative. Instead of spending money for a bathtub faucet, I used standard pipe fittings and valves. The cost in materials was $12 instead of $180. Retro is in, and using old sinks and faucets from the building would be more fashionable than trying to buy new ones.

I've also done things not to code. In one studio, I wanted a water supply near my painting area, but there was no drain or vent within a hundred feet. So I ran a small cold water line to where I wanted it, added a standard shutoff valve, and put a bucket under it. I had a grocery cart, and the wastewater was pushed to my sink a hundred feet way. I had clean water when I needed it, and at the end of the day it was not that much of a deal to wheel the bucket to the utility sink, since I had to clean my brushes anyway.

Toilets are so cheap that it is usually cheaper to buy a new toilet than to deal with what might be wrong with an old one. If you have a building where restrooms came with two toilets, you can remove one toilet and easily install a shower in its place.

Most important is to place new plumbing close to existing vent lines, so you don't have to add a lot of expense by running new vents through the roof. Talk to some plumbing contractors before you set your plans in stone.

Finally, if you are going to have a plumber there, or if you have to run a new drainpipe, think ahead. You may want to run a four-inch drain line to accommodate a toilet someday, even if you are only putting in a sink for now. In one building, each studio had sinks, but I envisioned artists wanting full bathrooms someday, so we roughed in the drains that way. Sure enough, ten years later, each studio had been transformed that way.

Windows. Windows in an industrial building can be a large item - literally. In our mill, the windows are about five feet wide by eight and half feet tall. Each window is divided into 25 to 30 panes. There are more than 10,000 panes of glass to worry about.

If windows are in poor shape, they can be replaced or repaired. Replacement windows will run several hundred dollars each, but they will be weather sealed and have thermal glass.

More economical is to learn how to repair a window. You can hire and teach someone at minimum wage. One window can be repaired in about a day; working fast, you might get two windows done in a day. Basically, the window has to be removed and put on a table or sawhorses, the old glass removed and new putty and glass put in. Then the window has to be painted on both sides, cleaned and reinstalled. Before reinstalling the window, the frame should be painted.

Old windows really should have a second layer for winter insulation. One solution is to purchase large sheets of Plexiglas (about 1/4 inch; you may get away with 3/16) and screw the Plexiglas to the inside frame around the window. If you drill holes in Plexiglas, be sure to use a bit made for plastics and either use rubber washers or use a countersink (larger) bit to enlarge the top part of the hole. If you don't, a tightened screw can crack the Plexiglas. You can also use twist brackets to hold the Plexiglas in place. Be prepared to spend quite a bit for the plastic when using large sizes.

In one building, the old windows were not salvageable. Today, I would probably order replacements, but at that time, a carpenter figured he could make custom-designed windows. My ingenious observation was to note that, even in the warmest days of summer, rarely were all windows opened. So we made custom windows for every other window. The windows we skipped were filled with large sheets of clear Plexiglas that were easily attached with trim. The same amount of Plexiglas was used as for the custom windows, but it was ordered to size, and with a quick installation, and by skipping the custom windows, a lot of money was saved while letting in a lot of light.

Insulated plastic (polycarbonate) sheets of Lexan by GE Plastics can be used if you want a translucent look and better insulation. Glass block can fill window openings, but it is much more expensive.

For fast repairs, we use silicone to adhere patches of translucent Cor-x plastic (see materials section), which can be cut to size with a razor blade. It does the trick until the window can be removed and a proper repair made.

Windows are targets for kids with stones. However, if you make your presence known in the area, they will find another abandoned target. In the Washington warehouse building, a lot of thought was put into whether to repair the old windows or install new ones. One big consideration was the neighborhood. I decided keeping glass windows would mean more breakage. In the mill, however, this wouldn't be possible with thousands of panes of glass. Once the mill became active again, breakage went down from the hundreds to less than six a year. Small towns are a bit easier than rough, urban neighborhoods. We also make sure that there are no small stones anywhere near the building.

Security. Studios are often in bad neighborhoods. It is important to keep your tenants, visitors and yourself safe, as well as the contents of the building. When people see TVs and computers going into a place, it becomes a temptation.

When I converted the Washington, D.C., warehouse, I decided not to overly advertise the new use. Although the new windows obviously showed improvements, they were painted a conservative dark brown and the exterior brick was left alone. Not only did I want to downplay the studios locally, but why give the city an excuse to raise the appraisal, which then increases real-estate taxes.

Doors should be secure with good locks, and you should install an intercom system where visitors and delivery people must announce themselves. Leaving doors ajar for an expected visitor is a bad habit. Certainly, bars and reinforced door edges help give protection. The addition of a security alarm sticker, whether or not it is really activated, also helps.

You should walk around the property and pretend you want to break in. Look for weak areas. Does the garage door not go all the way down, so there is room to crawl underneath it? Can the lock be picked with just a credit card? Unfortunately, if you do have an intercom with a remote door opener, the lock won't be as secure as a dead bolt.

Some people will try to break in because they think there are valuables inside; others will break in because they see an opportunity, like a door or window left open; and others will break in because they are high on drugs and it won't make any difference what is inside; there will be no logic.

It might pay to have a security system installed. You can get some, under maintenance contracts, that will automatically call the police. I had one, and the only time someone, either drunk or high on drugs, set it off, he had time to go through the building and climb out a rear window with some bizarre takings, before the police finally showed up. Today, there are dozens of products on the market that you can install yourself. If you get one that makes a lot of noise, you will probably be protected from most dangers.

The point is that, while it's hard to prevent bizarre break-ins, you can prevent 95% of them.

Make sure all tenants know when doors should be locked, and that they should not be careless. In North Adams, you can leave tools outside and go to lunch. In Washington or New York, if you turn your back, the tools are gone. Know your neighborhood and adjust accordingly.

I've found that women especially are concerned, rightfully so, and steps should be taken at least to minimize the potential for crime.

Finally, I cannot emphasize enough that everyone should take an active role. I've seen city blocks turn ugly in a matter of a couple of weeks. If a streetlight goes out, people will begin to do drugs or urinate in the street, trash will be thrown, and the next thing you know, you have yourself a minor slum.

If you see a light out, call the electric authority immediately; keep trash picked up, and chase vagrants away. Get it known that your building is active and you won't tolerate questionable behavior. If there are other problems, call the police and the mayor's office. The more you make noise, the sooner you will get action.

I also believe in paying a few dollars to have local residents do small jobs, like shoveling snow or sweeping the front. You don't want to invite them into the building to inspect all your valuables, because even if they are honest, they will gossip about your 'art' building. But it pays to make friends and to become one of the community. Locals rarely rob neighbors, unless everyone is in the 'business.'

Floors. If you have concrete floors, leave them. If you have wood floors in bad shape, find out if you can peel off a layer or whether you need to screw a new layer on top. If your floors are uneven, often you can live with them. They become less of an issue as your space fills up. It is far better to build a new floor in one critical area than to worry about the entire floor space.

In many loft buildings, prior manufacturing processes have left thick layers of glue and other coatings. It is a back-breaking job of scraping, sanding, chiseling, applying paint removers (deadly vapors) and, as one advisor said, "doing whatever it takes" to get down to the original wood floor, which then can be fine-sanded and clear-coated. My guess is that, unless your needs are really to be a 'design loft,' you won't need to bother to beautify the floors to this degree.

Often just painting the floors can dramatically make the difference. You don't even have to have special paints. (See Building Materials: Paint.)

Wafer board, particleboard, Masonite or plywood make great, fast floor coverings. Thicker sheets will hide a lot of imperfections.

I am a strong believer in contrast. In one studio, I built a twenty-by-twenty-foot platform about one foot high and this became my office area. Not only did the extra height give me a nice view of the remaining space and allow me to see out the windows from a sitting position, but the contrast made the rough wooden floor around the platform seem that it was left on purpose and not just to save money.

Walls and Ceilings and Beams. You might be tempted to sandblast, but you might find this an impractical proposition because of lead in the paint. Instead, just clean off the old paint the best you can with a scraper and leave it. If it bothers you, then paint over it (see below).

Exposed bricks can also be left alone. For a studio space, I wouldn't bother sealing them with a clear coat. You can clean brick with a variety of products, and you can also rub on thin layers of new paint to give it a fresh look. Ceilings might have a variety of insulation already installed. Leave it; it probably has a value being there. You can always install an additional layer of sheetrock for cosmetic reasons.

Beams usually are neat-looking if left alone. There is a tendency to try to hide them in new walls, but after a while, you will find that they look great randomly placed near new partitions.

Plaster may be damaged, but you can patch it easily. If you have bumpy or cracked plaster walls and ceilings, one technique is to simply take a very wide trowel and use drywall compound. Spread it on thin like butter, and then scrape off as much as you can. Sand lightly, and once it's painted it will look as good as new.

Painting. Years ago, I bought a secondhand professional paint sprayer. The sprayer was rated 1 1/4 GPM. GPM stands for gallons per minute. I can spray the contents of a five-gallon bucket of paint in just four minutes.

I've used the sprayer to paint hundreds of linear feet of wall. I can paint a wall ten feet high by fifty feet wide, for example, in about ten minutes. The problem with spraying houses or finished areas is that you need to mask or protect areas from the overspray. In a large industrial space, you have less to worry about. Ceilings, walls, floors, ductwork – almost anything can be sprayed quickly.

Go to a few paint stores and get prices on paint by the five-gallon bucket. Because you are spraying, you really don't have to be concerned about the quality. Buy the cheapest paint you can get. At the same paint store, you can probably rent an airless spray gun unit. Then go to town.

There's nothing like a nice clean coat of paint to make you forget the somewhat dirty history that an industrial building may have. You really don't want to get into sandblasting because of dust and lead issues, so painting is the way to go.

When you have a space of fifteen thousand square feet, for example, just mopping the floor can be a major chore. Construction will add up the longer it takes. That's why I like to get in and get it done fast. I am less concerned about how pretty things are, because I figure I can touch up and add some nice details later. Painting with airless spray equipment is the only efficient way to go.

Elevator. It's great if you have a working elevator. But repairs are expensive, because they must be made by licensed contractors who charge at least $80 per hour, with two men usually calling.

Don't let an elevator become inactive. Once it has been out of service for a while, it must be renovated and brought up to new code, which could mean installing a new elevator. I will bet you that you will not be able to afford that.

Make sure that tenants don't abuse the elevator. In the multi-story warehouse studio building, I have an old elevator that still has pull cables instead of buttons. I had to seal in the shaft for fire codes, including installing metal doors, but I didn't have to change the guts of the elevator.

What gets my goat is when tenants use the elevator just because they are too lazy to walk up the stairs. If large or heavy supplies or artwork have to be taken up or down, I have no objection. But needless use will speed up the necessity of repairs. Lock up the elevator if you have to, and keep your license current. Otherwise, you will be liable if an accident happens.

Tenants will pay very low rents yet think that services should be the same as in an upscale new office building filled with law firms. Make your policy known.

Exterior. Leave things alone. Make changes after you've been there awhile. I've seen a lot of people spend too much energy and money on the exterior when it doesn't help the workspace. I know it's nice to have a cool-looking building, but it's better to concentrate on your priorities – on the inside, which will be used by you and others. Besides, by the time you've been there awhile, you will think of other ideas.

For the front of the Beaver Mill, where the Contemporary Artists Center had exhibition space open to the public, I bought three green market umbrellas, three tables, and twelve green plastic chairs. The three units altogether cost about $300 and made a better solution than any of the $3,000 suggestions. Besides, if you are doing an art building, you should be putting a sculpture outside.

Parking lots are quite expensive to resurface. Most likely, the arts use will need far fewer parking spaces than when the property was in full use. Dirt is a lot cheaper than asphalt. You might be able to use only a portion of the parking lot, and the areas that are broken up anyway can be covered with topsoil and grass seed. Obviously, this will add to your summer maintenance, but there may be an attraction in having a yard.

HAZARDOUS WASTES

If you have a serious hazardous waste problem, you didn't read and follow the first part of this manual. Be very, very careful about getting involved. I say this with experience although, in my case, I didn't follow this rule. I said be very careful, but I didn't say never.

In my case, I had a good indication that the previous owner would do - and had the deep pockets to carry it out - the remedial work on the mill. At the same time, my legal relationship was such that I did not take possession until the work was done. This was to protect me. Obviously, if all didn't go well, I would have lost quite a bit in my fix-up and time involved, but that would have been far and away better than declaring bankruptcy due to the cleanup costs involved. Luckily the previous owner did have the deep pockets, because several items that had to be cleaned up expanded into greater costs than were first estimated.

While I doubt that you will be dealing with these kinds of problems, I mention them for two reasons. One, many of the properties that don't sell are vacant because of hazardous wastes. These properties may look attractive at first glance, and so you may come across them. Second, some small properties could easily have problems. Gas stations and automobile repair shops are the most obvious examples.

Before you get involved with these kinds of properties, try to have someone pay for a professional survey.

Lead Paint. If you have an old industrial building, you undoubtedly have lead paint. Sandblasting it off is usually difficult, but get a price from a licensed contractor to do it in any case. Unlike residential properties, you don't have to remove it in commercial properties, because the government assumes that children are not going to be living in these spaces. Obviously, artists' lofts become exceptions. You will have to discuss this on an individual case-by-case basis. Often, if only adult artists will be living there as an accessory use, you won't have to remove any lead paint.

I prefer to get a nice, new coat of paint over all the old paint, unless enough natural brick shows so that I want to leave it alone. Cheap latex paint works fine, especially if you are spraying. If the paint is flaking away, then wear a mask and scrape it off as best you can. If scraping the paint creates dust, then you will have to consult with a licensed contractor, who can mask off the area and put in special ventilation while the work is being done. Also, check with that outfit or the health department regarding waste disposal. Then put on a heavy coat of new paint.

Asbestos. The most common problem you will deal with in an old building is asbestos. There has been a lot of noise about asbestos, but most of it concerns workers who used it in a manufacturing process day after day, and were exposed to the dust.

You will find asbestos wrapped around heating pipes and around boilers. If it is in good condition, you really don't have to do anything. However, because of all the press as well as state regulations, it will become a problem. Tenants will be afraid, and bank financing may be more difficult.

The other asbestos you might find will be in old, nine- inch-square floor tile.

The good news is that asbestos can be dealt with in a very straightforward manner. While you can hire a professional consultant, you can easily determine for yourself how much asbestos you have. Again, you can also call in an asbestos remover to give you an estimate. The contractor will tell you how much you have.

Pipe insulations can look alike, especially if they are dirty or have been painted. Asbestos around pipes is usually powdery if broken, compared to non-asbestos pipe insulation that usually has fiberglass inside the vinyl covering.

When you get an estimate for removal, the chances are you will be quoted $10 to $30 per linear foot for removal, depending on quantity. To repair the insulation might cost you 50% of this, so it is more prudent to spent more and get rid of it once and for all.

Asbestos removal must be done by licensed contractors, and you need to know their insurance and licenses, as well as their disposal destination.

Times can be slow for asbestos removers during part of the year. Even though 90% of the asbestos in my mill was in adequate condition and could have stayed, I had all of it removed for $4.50 per linear foot. It was done on a quantity basis, and it was done on the contractor's schedule. When he had other jobs to do, he didn't come. When he had a day or two of no work, he came and worked here. I didn't care, since it didn't disturb my work and since he was locked into a per linear foot rate.

It is worthwhile having asbestos removed and much more easily done when the space is empty and no tenants are around. Areas must be taped off and a special air ventilation/exhaust system put into place. Contractors - in special protective suits - then put a long sleeve of plastic sheeting around the pipe (ladders have to be placed under ceiling pipes to reach) and with gloves built into the plastic sleeve, the asbestos is removed into the plastic without ever allowing the dust to be exposed to the air.

If you have a lot of asbestos to remove, you can make up a schedule to do it over a period of years. Establish the priority areas to be done first, with asbestos in the worst condition, in areas that might interfere with rentals, or areas where living might occur.

Asbestos tile is another kettle of fish. If you have old, nine-inch floor tile, the chances are that there is some asbestos in the material. In most states, it can be thrown into a dumpster in large pieces. However, if it has disintegrated into small particles, then it must be removed and disposed of by a licensed contractor. The easiest way to deal with a tile floor is to just keep it and maintain it. Floors do not have the same psychological effect on tenants that pipe insulation has. Spending money to have the tile removed will leave you with a rough floor under the tile that then has to be covered. If you must do something, the cheaper solution is to install a new floor over the tile, leaving it sandwiched in between. We often use 4 x 8 foot sheets of wafer board (sometimes called OSB or Aspenite) or use particleboard, Masonite or plywood. These are normal materials found in all lumberyards and used for sub-floors. Normally, the material is put down and then a finished wood, tile, vinyl, or carpet floor is installed on top. But it looks neat as is, especially if coated with a urethane finish. The negative of wafer board is that the surface tends to "raise" with water, so if you are going to use water, then spend a bit more and put down plywood or Masonite. (Read the Building Materials chapter for tricks and more details.)

Oil and other Hazardous Wastes. In an old building, wear a mask, get a dumpster, and sweep up all the dirt and throw it out. If there are signs of real oil puddles (which should have been investigated before you settled), you need to find out what it is and get a licensed contractor to remove it. This can be expensive. In all probability, however, tiny bits of debris can just be removed. Use common sense. Obviously, if there are huge quantities of any material, you will have to ask specific questions about disposal procedures from a licensed contractor, the city health or building department or the waste disposal company. For normal cleaning, there are various granular materials you can buy (at janitorial supply stores) in buckets or barrels to help sweep up garage-type spaces.

CODE ISSUES

Communities may have different codes, especially regarding at what point 'public use' kicks in. It may be the kind of use or the number of people involved. You also may have a situation where you don't have to bring your property up to code because you are grandfathered in, but my philosophy is that you should try to adhere to these principles, no matter how few people are involved. There are some generally accepted codes throughout the United States:

Fire exits. Make sure that each tenant has two means of egress. Doors to private studios must open inward, so they don't open and block the hallway where people may be rushing to exit a building on fire; all hallway and entrance doors have to be made to open outward to allow people in a panic to flee (that's why, in public spaces, the bar opener on the door is called a 'panic bar.' Even in private buildings, the doors cannot have a lock that requires a key from the inside. However, you can still use normal entrance locks that require a key from the outside, and therefore will prevent someone from coming in.

Many codes will require UL-listed metal or solid wood doors. You can sometimes pick up used metal doors for a third of the price of new ones. If you are building a public space, such as a performance space, you may have to install push (panic) bars on the doors.

Emergency Lighting Systems. An emergency lighting system is required so that, if the electricity fails during a fire, the lights come on, powered by batteries, to allow people to have enough light to exit. They are not expensive, and you can buy them at most building supply stores as well as from electrical suppliers.

Handicapped Access. This is not necessary unless you are changing the space for public use. It's not a bad idea, however, to build handicapped access in any case, because you never know what the future will bring. Generally, ramps cannot rise more than one foot for every twelve feet of length. Doors have to be at least 32 inches wide (they should be much wider to accommodate artwork), and hallways should be five feet wide to allow two wheelchairs to pass each other. The good news is that whatever helps to make your building accessible is also a wise move to support the various art operations. Wide sculptures and paintings are more bulky than wheelchairs. The National Endowment for the Arts has a handbook for accessible arts programming called <u>The Arts and 504</u>, which gives additional details in a simple form.

Firewalls. Check about fire codes in your community. You may be required to have a fire barrier between spaces, and certainly, if you have a hallway, you must have a fire barrier. The principle is that someone who leaves the premises during a fire should have two ways to get out of the building. Whichever route is chosen, that hallway should be lined with a fire barrier (in most cases a two-hour barrier, which means that the materials used have been tested and it takes at least two hours for a fire to burn through the material). In many cases, 5/8-inch sheetrock is accepted. So when you have a choice of which thickness sheetrock to use, you might want to spend a little more to satisfy this code.

PUBLIC RELATIONS

Labor. Throughout most of this book, I have made indications that you should shop around for prices. Different contractors will give you differing advice as well as estimates. I've seen estimates swing as wide as from $2,000 to $20,000 for the same work. For an industrial space, you will always pick the $2,000 bid.

Undoubtedly, you will do some of the work by yourself or with friends. Then there will be a large group of people who will want to do the work moonlighting.

Be forewarned that, if you hire people during evenings or weekends, you are taking a chance. If you own property, you now have assets. If anything should happen and a person gets hurt, he/she could sue you for damages. In addition, the IRS will come after you for not paying payroll taxes and filing properly. There is a host of consequences that you will not want to experience.

Even homeowners who hire neighborhood kids to cut their grass during the summer months are taking a chance. I'm not saying that people don't do it and get away with it, but I would suggest a different solution.

Most tradespeople who moonlight like to be paid in cash, because they don't want to report it to the government and pay taxes on it. However, you can offer them 20% more in wages, and that should cover their taxes. It does not pay for you to lose sleep over the possibility of getting into trouble. If you are spending $50,000 to fix a studio building, add $2,000 to the cost to cover this type of expense.

My suggestion is to think of labor in the building the same way you think of labor in the studio. Whenever you need help, why take a chance? Set up an account with a payroll service, take down an employee's name, address, social security number, and number of exemptions – and let the payroll service report and file all necessary forms and taxes. It will cost you, but you can spend your time saving money elsewhere.

If you hire people to do a substantial amount of work, and they work for you as independent contractors, they should have their own workers' compensation insurance. Get their social security numbers or federal ID numbers and let your accountant file 1099 forms for them. The government is cracking down and it's best to be clean.

I've also seen people hire their friends and pay cash. Everything goes fine until one of the employees gets hurt, or has some bad financial luck and decides to file for unemployment benefits anyway, naming you as the employer. Don't think that, just because you're friends, someone won't try to slam you. I once hired a part-time person for a few weeks. He then left to work somewhere else full time. Eventually, he was laid off that job. When he filed, he tried to receive unemployment compensation from me, I guess because he couldn't get it from his new employer. He didn't get it, but it was good that I had reported his wages, nonetheless.

Finally, sometimes artists try to go around tax codes, even as employers do. As I've said many times, if you are smart and dedicated in your art, you probably won't be paying taxes. Between write-offs to which you're entitled as a result of dealing with an old building and write-offs as a result of the operation of an art studio, you will have many legitimate losses to offset your income.

Neighbors. Get to know your neighbors. They may be interested in knowing about you. If you are doing work in a building tenanted by others, sounds and odors travel.

If you need to work late with unusually loud tools, talk to anyone who might be disturbed. It is better they see you personally than call the police. One tenant coated her studio floor with clear polyurethane in preparation for moving in. She didn't provide sufficient exhaust fans, and people upstairs had to vacate for the day. Needless to say, it was not a great way for her to introduce herself.

Most of these problems can be avoided with person-to-person communication. One way or another, doing construction will be a nuisance to someone nearby. It is almost impossible to prevent this. It is always better and cheaper for you to take a preventive measure than to deal with it afterwards. Even so, you may not be able to satisfy everyone, but at least you can say that you made an effort.

SCHEDULING

Coordinate the Work. If you rush, you will pay more. Often you can get contractors to lower the price if they can work it into their schedules. I've done this, but usually I find that it costs me more money. Delays with one contractor will delay others. You, meanwhile, are paying for the building and not using it.

It is important, however, to know what each trade is supposed to do. Carpenters build the wall studs, and then electricians and plumbers run their pipes and wires in the wall and through the studs. Then you will probably have to get an inspection before you can close in the walls with sheetrock. After the sheetrock has had tape, joint compound, and paint, the electrician comes back in to install fixtures and cover plates on switches and outlets, and the plumber comes in to install the sinks and toilets and other fixtures. Then it might be time for carpet or other types of flooring treatment, installation of equipment, and final touches. Obviously, prior to some work, you may have to deal with fire systems, concrete, roof, window and other repairs. Write down all the work in a schedule to give yourself an idea of how it will work. Then make the contractor stick to the schedule. I have spent a lot of time nagging people. A delay could have repercussions down the line.

If you have a bank construction loan, often the loan payments are made in installments that are tied to what work has been completed. The bank wants to avoid lending the money with the expectation that it will have a renovated asset as collateral, only to find that the money has been spent, the contractors have not been paid, and the work is a long way from completion. Typically, you might get one third up front, one third after all the rough-in has been completed, and the remaining third when the work is done and you've gotten your certificate of occupancy.

You want to do the work in all the areas that you committed to, because otherwise the bank may not release the money to you. This causes more stress, because contractors are nagging you for their payments. Often their cash flow is not great, and they need the money to pay their workers.

I recommend that, once the work is underway, you do it continuously without rushing. But I also recommend that you sometimes put off doing work. You can also divide up the construction into areas. Perhaps you will deal with one floor first, and after that is completed you will do the second floor. Obviously, if you need to install a panel box that will feed the entire space, you will keep both projects in mind and get the size that will handle it all. If wires have to feed through the studs in order to get them to the upper floor, do that also. But from experience I know that, if you can tackle one big project a year, sometimes the entire complex does not have to be done the way a well-endowed museum might do it.

CHAPTER 7
Building Materials

You can have your own oasis inside your warehouse.

ELEMENTS AND MATERIALS

Plastic Sheeting. Don't overlook the obvious. Plastic sheeting is sold at all lumberyards. It comes in rolls up to 100 feet long and as wide as 20 feet. I hang it by stapling it along a beam or the ceiling to make temporary curtains/partitions during construction, and permanently to separate areas from dust. It's quick and effective and cheap.

I also stretch clear plastic around lightweight frames that serve as standing walls, allowing light to pass through and heat to stay in. These walls can then be moved during summer or when I need to move out a large sculpture.

Floors. You've read already that I am a believer in wafer board (also called OSB for Orion Strand Board and Aspenite) that comes in various thicknesses in four-by-eight- foot sheets. Leaving it as a finished floor gives a neat look. You can also use A/C (smooth on one side) plywood or Masonite as a finished floor.

Paint can be used with all kinds of techniques and I've described some ideas below.

Shop around for carpet and question installers. It is a fast solution, especially for areas where you want an office finish. You can buy direct from some manufacturers (you are an "art design" business, after all) and S & S Carpet (800-241-4013) specializes in direct sales to customers. Once we got dozens of carpet samples and odd pieces of carpet, and put them down to form a large jigsaw carpet. If you shop for carpet, ask only for roll prices, not cut prices.

Vinyl tile and sheet goods, as well as real ceramic

tile or slate, are expensive and probably not applicable for large spaces, unless you want to use some in one tiny area just for an accent.

I've seen people who have found a cache of lumber, especially barn boards and old planking, and then nail that down as a new floor. It all depends on what you can find.

Concrete can be poured, but that's a rather labor-intensive job. But again, you might want to do a small area for accent, especially if the truck is coming to pour foundations or for other repairs.

Other solutions have included just building a platform in different tiers on top of an old floor. Sometimes if you need a level floor and the old floor won't suffice, it's easier to simply ignore it and go on top with something new.

Faux floors of all styles are possible. You can use clear polyurethane to imbed all kinds of materials. For example, brown paper can be ripped into flagstone shapes, adhered to the floor with paint or polyurethane, and then clear-coated with polyurethane to seal it in. Use your imagination; you can use almost anything - from newspapers to rejected artwork.

Most artists want to keep the original wood floors. Then you find out how much fun sanding is. Like mowing a lawn a hundred times, it's monotonous work. You can rent heavy-duty sanders at most paint or hardware stores. You'll need a small sander to do edges and corners. After using three grades of sandpaper, from rough to finish, you'll need to coat the floor. Otherwise, the nice new wood will look terrible in a few months. The most common coating is clear polyurethane. Put on three coats and your floor will last for years.

Paint. Paint can do wonders for anything. If you have the worst-looking mishmash of brick, wood and plaster with many angles and cracks, try a deep color of paint and it will all disappear, especially if you add an adjacent wall that is smooth and pure white.

Top-of-the-line paint that is returned to Wal-Mart goes back to the manufacturer, who dumps it into one vat and makes a gray paint that is poured into two-gallon buckets and sent back to Wal-Mart to be sold for $6.00 per two-gallon pail. For $3.00 a gallon, you are buying good quality paint, but in one color. I've used it for everything, including floors and walls and roofs. In one space, the plywood floor was a mess, and I didn't have much money or energy to tackle the job. In two hours I painted the floor gray, then took a thin brush and painted in white lines to represent the mortar around flagstones. The faux flagstone was quite a hit. Sometimes the easiest and cheapest way out is the best one.

Wal-Mart sells a five-gallon pail of flat, interior latex for under $20. You may find similar bargains at other stores. No need to spend a fortune on paint - especially if spraying - for industrial walls. A few crisp walls of white or some color can offset the dark, dreary walls of an old building and bring it all to life. Color the doors, railings, ductwork, beams, pathways on the floor, and sectionalize or delineate areas by using a different color.

Cor-x. This material looks like a plastic cardboard. It comes in colors and 'clear,' which is really a translucent, allowing light to go through. It's about $15 per 4 x 8 foot sheet, so it is very economical. Sign companies use it a lot to attach vinyl letters. Look for it at sign supply or plastic supply companies.

We use it a lot to patch windows. Patches can be made in seconds by adhering it with clear silicone. Although it tends to get brittle after a few years, it still is the best patch one can make for the time involved.

I also use it to cover windows during the winter for insulation. I can always use clear Plexiglas on one or two windows in order to keep viewing possible, but the others can be covered with Cor-x. Sheets can be stapled up and taken down in seconds and stored for the next season.

At the sleek offices of a special-effects film company and at the new MASS MoCA offices, partitions are made of twin-celled sheets of Lexan that are screwed to metal studs. It's a neat system where electrical wires are somewhat visible. You can do the same for a fraction of the cost by using Cor-x.

I also use the material for a number of other applications, including for my art. MASS MoCA used it for an exhibition by simply hanging sheets of it from the ceiling with wire. You can take clear plastic wrapping tape and tape several sheets together. Keeping several sheets on hand will not be a waste.

Polyurethane Foam. I buy foam in 55-gallon drums and use industrial equipment to spray polyurethane foam for my sculptures, so perhaps I'm biased. You can get foam in spray cans for as little as $2 in almost all hardware, lumber and all-purpose stores. Even with all my equipment, I buy the cans and use them a lot. The foam can't be beat for insulating and sealing up large holes around pipes.

One trick, which shows how you can spend very little to get satisfactory results, is to use it to fill holes in floors. Often floors have many holes where pipes used to run. Traditionally, rather than nailing over the hole with a metal patch, one would find a large wood dowel, cut it to size and pound it in, then sand it down to the floor finish. Instead, I use tape or stuff some paper in the hole (to prevent the foam from just leaking through), and spray a "puff" of foam into the hole, filling it only about halfway. Let it expand and set up for a couple of hours. The foam will expand into a big blob and more than fill the hole. Then take a carving knife and slice the foam at the floor level. You really don't need to do anything else; if you want to match it closer to the floor color, then paint it. You can walk on it and it will hold up just fine. Prepare all the holes that you need to fill, then do them quickly, all at one time, because usually when you set the can down for a while, it gums up and you can't get more out.

Sometimes you find interiors with cheap-looking paneling. The best solution is to sheetrock over it. I've also used drywall compound to fill in the grooves and then painted them smooth. The problem is that the paneling might be flexible, and this will cause the compound to crack. One trick is to drill small holes, and then squirt some foam (via a straw that comes with the can of foam) into each hole. It will foam a mass, and hold the paneling firm. (A soda can filled with foam cannot be crushed.)

Concrete. Good old concrete is heavy but cheap. For an industrial look and to save buying expensive marble, granite or plastic countertops, we poured concrete on top of a plywood base with temporary thin metal edges, and we now enjoy a smooth slab of concrete for our kitchen island and counters. With a sealer coat, it is just as good as a slab of stone.

While we were making a mess pouring the concrete, we also poured an inside patio where the floor was very uneven. We made and leveled a grid out of 2 x 4 lumber, and poured the concrete in the square openings, then left the concrete and the lumber together, which formed the grid pattern. With two garden tables, market umbrellas and chairs, it feels like an outside patio right inside our space, especially with the two $30 ceiling fans cooling things down during summer months.

We also poured a few other slabs that served as sculpture bases. Once you are pouring, it doesn't take much more effort to add some more details. You might have to pour to repair a floor segment; since the truck is coming, that would be the perfect opportunity to include some design features as well.

Exposed Conduit, Ductwork, Pipes. It is only my aesthetic opinion, but exposed electrical conduits and heating ducts (especially round ones) are beautiful by themselves and do not have to be hidden. Exposed utility lines are cheapest to install, repair and deal with. When you see exposed ducts in the fanciest and trendiest of stores and eateries, you know that you too can stay trendy and save money. Many of the fashion trends of recent years have originated out of artists' functional studio spaces.

If you need to install new ductwork, check the prices for round duct versus rectangular duct. It's more attractive and perhaps only a bit more in price. Labor is the same.

Finally, you will spend a lot of time trying to figure out how to install pipes within walls so they won't be seen. It's a natural tendency if you have had any experience with normal residential renovation. Don't worry about it. Just let the pipes go where they have to go for the cheapest way out. When it is all concluded, and all your art is in the loft, you won't even notice the pipes anymore.

Loft patio with concrete poured in a wood grid.
Keep it simple with your work areas, but jazz up your residential loft.

Lighting. Lighting is so important that various light systems have been described in the construction section. However, there are some tricks I've observed. For accents, one artist bought copper pipe and ran wires and drilled holes so that every four feet a simple bulb and tin cover fixture hung down. It looked as nice as any track-type system but it was just put together with a few industrial materials.

A great trick that MASS MoCA used before they had their finished space was to move the eight-foot-long fluorescent fixtures to the tops of the crossbeams rather than have them hang under the beams. The few hours it took to do this gave the ceiling a dramatic look as the light was directed upward. A few spots were aimed at sculptures, but with all the normal lights hidden, the overall effect was great.

I did a similar thing for our group dining room. The sandblasted brick and exposed beams and ceiling had a great look, but the ceiling was too low to hang fixtures. There was a deadline to get the space ready, so I simply had the five fluorescent fixtures hung on the side facing away from the entrance. It gave a great light from one side, and from the other it looked as if Dan Flavin had stopped by.

And to emphasize again, the cheapest conduit and

light holders, left exposed and using exposed floods, have a nice look. There's no need to spend more money.

Window Shades. Large windows should just be left alone when possible. Simply white cotton cloth or gauze can be used as shades. Attach the cloth to strips of wood and hang it on two hooks/nails or stretch it around thin stretchers and hang the frame or screw it to the inside window frame. The soft light and tight, stretched cloth gives off a nice effect.

I buy white "bamboo" shades that are really plastic. You can get them five feet wide, and on sale they are around $8.00. Cor-x can be used to give privacy but allow light. Window shades and blinds can be bought cheaply, although the size limitations may not work for large, industrial windows.

Sheetrock. Sheetrock or drywall or wallboard or gypsum board (they are the same) is very inexpensive. It comes in 4 x 8, 4 x 10 and 4 x 12 (foot) sheets. It is usually anywhere from 3/8 to 5/8 inch thick. One-half inch is the most common, except for fire-protected sheetrock, which is 5/8 inch thick. Installed in a few minutes, it covers studs and gives you a solid plane.

Sheetrock can be cut to size with a razor blade. Score one side of the paper cover, bend it and then cut from the other side. It's very quick.

The best way to install it is to use a screw gun with drywall screws. You can also nail, but it's a bit messier and then you can't take it down. For studio space, there's no need to put drywall tape and compound on the joints, or compound to cover the screw heads and then to paint it. Just leave the natural gray/brown paper finish. It might fade a bit under daylight, but I've left it as is in many studio areas for at least a decade or two and it still looks fine. There are tricks to getting nice edges top and bottom, by using trim or j-bead, or leaving it a couple of inches off the floor. Look around at galleries for ideas. If the floor is very uneven, hang the sheetrock with the bottoms level, starting at the highest point on the existing floor. Paint the gap between the wall and the floor black, or just let the studs show naturally, and the wall will float over the floor, leaving perhaps several inches between the bottom of the wall and the lowest point of the floor.

I've used sheetrock for sculpture platforms where not a lot of weight would be put on it; for some platforms, I've used it on top of rough plywood just to get a smooth skin. Corners are finished with corner-bead, which also can be left exposed.

Although not easy to lift unless you rent a scissors lift or scaffold, or build long 'T' supports (make a support by nailing a four-foot 2 x 4 to the end of a 2 x 4 long enough to wedge between the floor and the ceiling), sheetrock can cover a ceiling quickly. Once you have two or three screws to hold it in place, you can screw the rest. As for walls, make sure the sheetrock edges line up with the middle of the studs or beams. Screws are put on both edges and in the middle area wherever you have studs.

Wall Tricks. Studs are usually placed 16 inches apart, although sometimes you will build walls with studs 24 inches apart if the wall isn't needed to support weight. You can lay the 2 x 4s on the floor to build your wall. Take your top and bottom 2 x 4 lengths and put them together. Then make marks every 16 inches. Move the two lengths apart and set in your studs. Nail them using two nails at each end where you made marks. Stand up your wall, and nail into place. Try to make walls conform as best as you can to the size of sheetrock. Use the same technique for metal studs, only use screws instead.

I often make walls ten feet high regardless of the much higher ceiling height. You can have the studs on the ends go all the way up to attach the wall to the ceiling, or perhaps it will be supported by being attached to another wall at the edge. In either case, if you don't need 100% privacy, usually ten feet is high enough to separate areas and prevent activity on one side from interfering with life on the other side. This also allows heat to flow to both sides.

If you are dividing up spaces to rent out, planning your partitions will be more contingent on heating and security issues. You can construct your partitions so that they touch (and are attached to) the undersides of the beams, allowing a few inches of opening at the top. It still allows air and noise to go through, but with high walls there is still privacy and it has a clean look.

Once you've built the basic walls, you can also cut out openings in various shapes and leave them open or put in Cor-x or glass to allow light to go through.

Insulate the walls if heat or sound might be a problem. It is much easier to do it now than later, and it shouldn't add that much more to the cost. I've made the mistake of rushing walls and then having to deal with tenants' complaints about the radio habits of their neighbors.

You can build round walls by cutting out of plywood your top and bottom plates (attach a pencil to a long string with the other end nailed temporarily, then use the pencil to mark your arc like a compass), then nailing in studs just as you would do a flat wall but along the curved plates. Take a thinner sheet of sheetrock and dampen it with a wet sponge and slowly let it bend around your curve. After screwing it in place, take another layer of sheetrock and do the same, making sure the edges do not line up with the edges of the sheetrock below. Homosote sheets will also bend, and you can use them instead of drywall.

In one building where the ceiling was dusty and I wanted a clean work area, we screwed sheetrock to the ceiling. Rather than cover the entire room, we covered just the area above the table and finished it with compound and white paint. The workspace just under this area was clean, and it gave the entire space a nice look. By the way, ceiling joists are often uneven in old buildings because the builders only cared about leveling the lumber to receive the floor above. Don't think you have to shim and level the ceiling in order to install sheetrock. Once painted, the high ceiling will hide how uneven it is. You mostly notice uneven ceilings when they are low and you can eyeball them at a low angle.

Don't forget to consider other materials for walls. Metal studs are about the same price as lumber, and faster to assemble than lumber. You need to get some tin snips and learn the tricks. It won't take long. The walls seem flimsy at first, but it's really the sheetrock that holds them together. Some building codes require metal studs for commercial buildings.

Try to make translucent walls with Cor-x and put internal Christmas lights in the walls for a great effect. You can also find other materials to use. Fiberglass roofing (curvy zigzag, three-foot-wide sheets, up to twelve-foot lengths, in colors and translucent) that is normally used for patio covers and roofing sections can be used as finished walls. It's pretty inexpensive. In fact, metal roofing is also a great look for any vertical surface, inside or out. They sell a foam insulation that is covered with an aluminum foil. It's soft, but maybe you want it to pin drawings on or use it for ceiling insulation as well. Go to your suppliers and look around.

Where privacy is not an issue, you can use outdoor chain link fencing, with associated gates. They used this in warehouses to lock up valuables, but the new, galvanized metal has a 'retro' look.

Shelves, Counters and Partitions. Look for industrial shelves. You can place them around like walls. In one case, I bought a building that had quite a few large, heavy wooden shelf units – almost like a library. I removed every other one, and created bays for working. Then I installed sheetrock on one side of the shelf unit or the other, so that every bay had some shelves and some wall space. There was no need to build separate dividing walls.

Never too many shelves: find industrial leftovers or build them.

Scrounge around for companies that are closing, for big items like metal shelves, desks, partitions, chairs, tables and other furniture.

One artist took all the old doors from the building and made counter bases and partitions with them. In contrast with the new walls, they looked great.

Flexible Hose. Computers are being used more and more. In one high-tech computer graphics office, they hung regular flexible vacuum cleaner hose that can be purchased from a variety of distributors, and put all of the computer cables through them. The exposed hose gave it a high-tech look and also made it very functional. Together with the lighted translucent walls, the office was great-looking.

Natural Light. Light is important. If you are lucky, you will have large windows. If you took over a warehouse that has a minimum of natural light, think about installing a major light source, either a large window or a skylight. A skylight can be made by framing a box and using twin-walled Lexan plastic sheet that comes in various sizes and looks like cardboard but blown-up. The air spaces act as insulation. Extra-large openings in exterior walls can be broken into sections and filled with a variety of window treatments.

One idea that can be dramatic, especially if you are in a bad neighborhood and you want to maintain the security of a closed building, is to cut open a large section of the roof, which will allow the weather to come in. Frame up around the area and you have a courtyard. If you have a two-story building, for example, put down flooring that can take water and add a drain and pipe it off under the floor to a regular drain. You can have your own oasis inside your warehouse. Add tropical trees and all of a sudden you have completely changed the character of the space.

Plants. Either you are a plant person or you are not, but to dramatically change industrial space from a design aspect, tropical trees will do it. They are a pain when you go away and have to have them watered, but they are the cheapest and most effective way of contrasting the industrial shell. Add a few smooth walls with large works of art, some furniture and drinks, and you will be in heaven.

Mail and Intercoms. I don't like many of the intercom systems I've found, but since you need something, get one that is inexpensive but at least covers all the tenants, with a few extra buzzers to cover future tenants. I have sometimes installed electric door locks, so that the entrance door can be unlocked by someone in the studio. Since industrial buildings are large, it is impractical to have to go all the way to the entrance to let someone in. On the other hand, you give up some security because these locks are not as good as deadbolts.

The modern types of mailboxes that you find in apartment buildings are rather expensive and seem unnecessary for many buildings, unless, of course, you are in a neighborhood where you have to go overboard with security. One solution I saw in a very fancy Internet-oriented office building was to use cheap metal mailboxes that you can buy at Wal-Mart for $5 each and line them up on a board. Having ten to sixteen on two rows can look neat, if you have the space. Talk to your local post office about what options they will tolerate and still deliver your mail.

CHAPTER 8
Equipment & Function

Make your studio space operational and serious.

I find it interesting when artists have studios in industrial spaces. They are, after all, manufacturing a product. While not being mass-produced, individual works hand-crafted reflect our industrial heritage. Studios in other types of buildings become funky, but there is a natural feeling when art is being made in former factories.

The studio should be considered as a factory, and the design and installation of equipment are to help the production run smoothly. The more artists think in manufacturing terms, the more effective their studio space will be.

Tools. For the studio operation and for running the building, you need basic tools. You should have at least the following tools, and in some cases have one per floor, especially large items such as ladders and vacuums. It takes too long to go downstairs to fetch an inexpensive tool not to have one nearby.

> Cordless screw gun/drill, with bits and screws
> Reciprocating saw (Sawzall), with metal blades
> Wet/dry shop vacuum with extension cord
> Push brooms, dustpans and lots of plastic trashcans
> Fire extinguishers
> Hammers, screwdrivers
> Ladders (each floor)
> Box of razor blades, scrapers, nails, screws
> Brushes, paint rollers and pans
> Sandpaper and sanding mop for drywall
> Level
> Staple gun and plenty of staples
> Measure tape (25-foot)
> Circular (skill) saw
> Cor-x, caulk gun and silicone
> Mop and bucket
> Flashlight and work light

With the above tools, you can fix and build most of what is needed, as well as take care of most emergencies. Obviously, an in-place table saw and a radial arm saw will help considerably if you have a lot of carpentry to do. Make it easy to carry your small tools around. Have a wheel cart if it works, or even a bucket. You can buy tool aprons that fit around five-gallon buckets.

Most of the 'tools' are really household items, but you want a super-large wet/dry vac rather than one you would buy for your house. Large studios generate a lot of dust, and without a doubt, this is also the best tool for cleaning up after a flood. A Sawzall (Milwaukee's brand name, but is commonly used for this type of saw regardless of manufacturer) is handy for getting through metal pipes and walls. If you do a lot of sheetrock work, then have a separate screw gun; otherwise a cordless drill will be fine.

In a working art building, the loading dock will be busier than the lobby.

Loading Dock. If you've acquired a building with a loading dock, congratulations. You will appreciate it more and more. Most industrial buildings have proper access for materials to be unloaded or loaded onto trucks. Art studios need the same type of access for materials. Few delivery trucks will have tail lift gates, enabling materials to be lowered to the street level. From building materials to raw materials for making art, the loading dock will be in constant use. One loading dock can be used by several studios and common space should be designed around this area.

If you've acquired a building without a loading dock, then think about purchasing a good forklift. Before I had a loading dock for my studio, I learned how to drop 55 gallon drums weighing 500 pounds off of trucks and onto automobile tires piled up. Believe me, I had nightmares about drums falling slightly off and rolling down the street instead. While it can be done this way, I would recommend using industrial equipment to help get heavy materials into the studio.

Woodshop. Most studios need some type of shop area, if not for wood, then for some other dirty process. You want to make sure you have adequate electricity, light, and ventilation as well as floor space for your operations and storage. You might be able to justify an expansion of your woodshop, because it can be used for the building's construction process prior to exclusive use for your studio. In fact, factor in the cost of a better-equipped shop when you figure in your construction expenses.

Think about dust and noise and access for supplies or finished products. Make sure this space is secure so that others will not have access without your permission. You will be surprised how many people come to you because your studio is so well equipped.

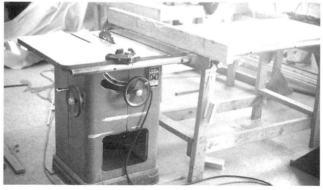

The table saw and woodshop should be centrally located.

Drawing Studio. Most visual artists need a good drawing table. Most people need some sort of worktable for projects. In many cases, this requires a big table. You could buy plywood and put it on two sawhorses and that would be quite adequate.

Masonite comes in 4 x 10 sheets up to one inch thick. (You may have to order it; you local lumberyard will not stock it this thick.) It's smooth, hard, long and heavy. It makes a wonderful tabletop.

I made a few tables with 1/2 or 3/4 inch, 4 x 8 foot, good-on-one-side (AC) plywood, so that one side could be raised like a traditional drafting table, only giant-sized.

Make sure you have extra-good light in this area. This is the place to spend just a little more to have the electrician wire up an overhead light.

Print Studio. If you are into printmaking or any operation where odors and vapors might be a problem, make sure you have a strong ventilation system. Keep all flammable materials, if not in a UL-listed cabinet (because OSHA will most likely not be visiting unless you have several employees), at least in some sort of metal cabinet. Keep fire extinguishers around. They are cheap, and when you need them, they are priceless.

From Harbor Freight, Northern Tools or a similar tool or auto supply store, you can get a parts washer sink for around $100. This re-circulates your cleaning solvent.

Painting Studio. For a painter, this is your main area. This is the heart of your studio. For a sculptor, a dancer, a filmmaker, the area I am talking about is where the bulk of your work is carried out. All other work radiates out from this activity.

Make sure you give yourself enough space. This is the reason that you have made such a big commitment. If it's supposed to be a messy activity, don't make a fuss about how it looks. But one lesson I've learned is that when you take over a big building, there will be many demands and you will find yourself too spread out. Sometimes I've not put enough resources into my own studio and later regretted it. This is your priority. Make sure others know it. Remember, although you might be spending a bit extra to outfit this space according to what you want, you will be using this space for many years. Averaged over this time period, it probably is not that much on a per-year basis.

Office Station. Computer, computer, computer. If you don't know how to use a computer, learn fast. You need it for all your operations, from letters to grant applications to accounting. Today, my recommendation is a laptop. If it seems strange that I'm giving advice to get a computer when this manual is about large studio spaces, it's because everything you do to run the building will flow through your computer – from leases, letters to banks (which have to look professional if you want the loan) to sending out invoices and keeping track of accounts. Add to the computer a fax, two phone lines with either a headphone or a neck support, printer, scanner and a good connection to the Internet. Your office and communication station is the nerve center for not only your studio operation but also for managing the property.

Telephone, Cable and Internet. Make sure you have sufficient lines into the building. If you are going to rent out spaces, put the terminal box in a common space so you don't have to be around every time the phone company comes to do work for some tenant.

Now is the time to ask about wiring up the building for the Internet. If you are renting to several tenants, ask if a T1 or DSL line would be economic. It will attract tenants. It can only go down in price, but right now in our region, a fast 768k DSL line can be installed for $300 per month. Divided up among a few tenants, it becomes a marketing tool as well.

Television cable companies may wire up your building for free, in anticipation of getting your tenants to sign up. There's little harm in getting them to invest in your property, and it's easier to do it in the beginning than later. At the very least, get them, along with the telephone company, to install panel boxes at a convenient location where they can get access for servicing and you can get access to pull lines to individual studios.

Storage. Everyone needs storage. Storage saves time because it is easier to put papers in a box and store it than to go through each paper and decide whether it needs to be saved or can be thrown out. If this sounds like I'm a pack rat and saving a lot of trash, my answer is that I'm too busy to waste time going through it all, and with a large building, another box or two that can hold hundreds of papers is the easiest way out. I mark the boxes with dates and generally what types of papers are inside. In case of a real need, I can always get into one. With high ceilings, they pile up to minimize wasted floor space. In a few years, if I want, I can throw them out without even looking at the contents.

The reason I have so many papers is partially due to having a large building. Operational papers simply accumulate. Keep receipts handy until you do your taxes, and for at least three years after that (the IRS recommends seven years).

For artwork, it pays to build proper storage shelves while construction is going on, and especially, to take advantage of high ceilings. Put away on the high shelves things you don't anticipate needing.

Display: You have a big studio building, and if you are professional, you will probably have people over to see your finished product, whether it's a painting, performance or film. Think about how you want someone to see it and how you can pull out requested work. You can also use a viewing space for other functions, such as photographing or videotaping your work.

Outside the creative aspect of the studio, you are building a professional workspace for the production of art. Like any business that manufactures a product, space is needed for related functions. Make your studio space operational and serious. The purpose of most businesses is to sell, demonstrate, display, and explain product to visitors. Think about how you want them to experience their time in your space.

If you have a wall or several walls where heavy works will be hung continuously, you might want to consider building them as a good gallery or museum would. On top of the studs, screw or nail a sheet of particleboard, wafer board or plywood. Then put your sheetrock on top. This method allows you to put a nail anywhere on the wall and get into wood. You won't have to worry about finding studs. To save on plywood, you can also put plywood at eye height, then fur out the studs to the same thickness with strips of plywood.

Office area in an artist's studio. Phone, fax and computer are essential.
(Photographer Andrea Haffner)

Kitchenette and Bathroom. Even if you are not living in your studio space, you still need to eat lunch and use the bathroom facilities. If you rent to others, you can have a common kitchen area, but that is not recommended. No matter how hard you try, you will not be able to get others to contribute fairly to keeping it clean. Also, you will find how incredibly messy some people are.

The same problem can occur to a lesser degree in bathrooms. When you select your tissue and paper towels, you may want to consider that artists who run out of paper towels in their personal studios will go to the public rest room and wipe out its paper towels. They will do the same with toilet tissue. One landlord got so upset with calls about no toilet tissue in the bathroom, he issued one roll of tissue per tenant per week and the tenants had to carry their own tissue when they used the rest room. I'm not suggesting you go that far, but as silly as it sounds, it can be a nuisance.

When You Need It. As was discussed in the construction section, fire is a major concern, especially for older buildings that were built with fewer fire-retardant materials in them. For your studio operations, you must think about getting proper ventilation fans. A twenty-dollar box fan perched on the windowsill will not suffice.

While you might not be able to afford the safety equipment large companies have working under OSHA rules, there are cheap substitutes. You might not have an emergency eyewash sink, but make sure you have a sink close enough, or a bucket of water. If you are working with flammable materials or chemicals, install proper metal cabinets as well as wipe-up materials. For example, I always have a bucket of sawdust to take care of any spills when using my polyurethane foam (in the liquid state before it mixes).

The main frustration you will experience if you have a large building, especially with more than one floor, is that every time you need something, you spend more time looking for it than it's worth. Many times we have driven down the road to the hardware store to buy an item rather than spend an hour looking for it. I have ladders, shop vacuums and hammers on each floor. It is essential to have these items accessible, and they can be replaced if people 'help themselves' since they are not expensive. Tools can be marked or color-coded to discourage their removal to private studios. A well-placed storage closet that can be locked is also a valuable addition, both for your working studio and for the building.

Odd and Ends. The more you observe what others are doing, the more tricks you will learn. If you need a dance floor, for example, you probably already know the various floors that are available. When you see something you need but don't have the budget, always ask what else can be used as a substitute.

Most artists come up with incredibly funky solutions to their needs. If you need a shower or tub, any container that can hold water and to which you can attach a drain will work. But if you are inspired to fashion a tub out of a child's wading pool with a shower hose above it, get the inspectors in and out of your building before you install these kinds of 'fixtures.' It will sidetrack their mission and you will become forever saddled with code issues. You might be able to classify these devices as 'temporary equipment.'

While I don't want to spend too much time on negatives, once in a while think about what can go wrong, and see if there are some easy steps you can take. A few extra fire extinguishers and medical kits are an inexpensive outlay. Besides, you should have these items during the construction stage in any case.

Finally, remember that we live in a disposable society, that businesses are changing all the time, either by going out of business or by adding new equipment to replace old. Take advantage of this and pick up free, used equipment and supplies. I used to remark that I could spend my entire day just driving around and getting free stuff, but I just couldn't take the time away from the studio.

CHAPTER 9
Operational Expenses

You'd better have a thick skin. You need to be mentally resistant. Keep in mind your own artistic ambitions.

HOW TO SAVE ON YOUR MONTHLY EXPENSES

This section deals with the month-to-month bills. Although life can really be quite simple – I write only about eight checks a month to take care of a 34,000 square foot building - the amounts on those checks can vary significantly if you are not careful.

I used to say that there is little difference in owning a house and owning a large, commercial building. You still need to call a roofer, an electrician, a plumber or a carpenter if anything goes wrong. You still need to write the same number of checks for utilities, mortgage and insurance. The only real difference is that the check amounts will be higher, and because you have many more plumbing and electrical fixtures, more heating units, more roof area, and more windows and doors, the chance of needing to make the call increases. Hopefully, you will be making deposits from rental income to cover these expenses.

Because expenses are therefore multiplied, it is very important that you get the lowest rates. You only have to negotiate once, not each time a service is performed. Once you have your electrician's hourly rate set, then if that service is needed, it will cost whatever the repair warrants. If you need gas, you only have to choose the company or plan that gives you the best buy. After that, it only needs to be monitored and perhaps reconsidered every year or two. The following will give you ideas on how to negotiate; believe me when I say that price proposals will vary all over the map, and the practical difference of choosing carefully can make or break your annual operation.

Gas. If you use gas, whether natural or propane, it will probably be for heat, since it seems to be cheaper and easier than oil or electricity.

Check around for rates. Deregulation has allowed more companies to offer the same product (as do telephone companies), and you won't know the difference, except that your bill can be up to 20% less. In a large building, that makes a big difference.

Gas rates are not like gasoline rates, where every time you drive down the street you can see big signs and compare prices. You really won't know if your supplier has upped the rates on your account, compared to a competitor, because prices go up and down all the time. You will have to call a competitor and ask what price they will give you for the amount of fuel you purchase over a year's time, then compare that price with your supplier the same week. Otherwise you won't know if there is a price difference, because of a change in their cost of fuel.

You will also have to determine who owns the meters, pipes, and, if you have propane, the tanks. Some companies make it very hard to switch.

Finally, try to find out the lowest rate you can get. Ask what the rate would be if you used more fuel. I've found, as one gas company manager told me right before I went after him for overcharging me, that it's like buying a car. No price is set until you make a deal. Find out their cost of fuel. In propane gas, a fairly good rate is to pay 30 cents over their cost for gas. Natural gas companies have fewer discount offers for quantity, but finding an alternative supplier might make a big difference.

Make it a practice to monitor the rates at least twice a season. Finally, and this advice may not hold up depending on energy needs, some companies lock into prices for the heating season, while others charge you a set amount over the cost of their gas, and their costs are in flux week to week. My inclination is to lock in for the season if you think the rate is reasonable, but it's a bit like predicting the stock market.

Electrical. Deregulation is the name of the game. Check around for the various rates that are offered, then all you have to do is let the company do the paper work.

Programs designed to lower your energy needs are very important. One electric company changed all the ballasts and every bulb in my mill and I only paid 20% of the cost, which they financed. That portion was paid in installments - added to my monthly electric bill over the course of two years. I couldn't even have bought new bulbs for that amount. Since the ballast is the bulk of a light fixture, it really was a good deal.

Energy companies will also come out and do free surveys of your energy needs and recommend ways you can insulate and change to energy-efficient fixtures. Don't take down lights until you've done this, because most programs are set up to change from inefficient to efficient fixtures, but they will not pay for new fixtures if none are there.

Certainly you can get rebates for buying energy-efficient, long-lasting light bulbs. Use lower-watt bulbs wherever you can get away with it, whether you buy through a program or just buy from a retail store.

Since motion detectors are so cheap, I use them for some hallways where traffic is infrequent and near outside entrances. That way, the lights come on only when needed.

Finally, save monthly expenses by making sure that your tenants are not wasting energy. Make sure your leases give you some leverage on this matter. Of course, it is better if they pay their own electricity so you don't have to worry about their carelessness.

Heating, Plumbing. The operation of the heating system is pretty straightforward. It is important to have a repair person on call. When something goes wrong, it is likely that it needs immediate attention. Floods or lack of heat are not problems to ignore.

Most heating systems do not need attention. If you have a hot-water boiler, you will need to empty a bucket of dirty water once a week. I do recommend highly that you get a timer control to adjust the boiler, geared to outside temperatures, and that you have a day cycle and a night cycle. The settings should be much lower for the nighttime use. You will never do as well manually, and the cost of the control will pay for itself back within months.

In plumbing, make sure you don't have leaks. Watch your usage carefully, because you will be surprised how much a small, running faucet can cost you.

You should learn to read meters and record the amounts down periodically. That way you will see when one meter increases. I keep tabs each year. Some bills will show your prior year's use, which is very handy to see if there is an increase without a reason. If it's not included, you can make the same determination by reading the meters yourself.

Small Emergencies and Repairs. Find the people who can do the little things as well as some carpentry. When something breaks, you can't always wait a week to fix it. If the front door won't close and lock, if a toilet is overflowing or if a roof is leaking around a flashing, make sure you have someone who can attend to it that day. It is worth paying extra for this service, because a minor item fixed early might prevent an even larger expense later on.

If you get comfortable and use only one firm for each trade, then you might be able to give them the keys so they will have access to public areas. This will save you time.

Make sure that you know where water shutoff valves are, and all electrical breakers. Absolutely buy from Sears their big, industrial wet vacuum. Always keep a 50 to 100-foot extension cord with it. It will save you during a flood, and will be indispensable for cleaning. Keep a ladder on each floor. Keep a mop bucket and mop handy as well. Keep a flashlight handy. Keep extra snow shovels and bags of sand and deicer. Go through the tool list and your supply list and make sure you stock the necessities. When you really need it, there might not be time to go to the store. Write your name all over the tools so they won't disappear into locked, private studios of tenants.

Trash. Use a dumpster service. It will also recycle. Try to get your tenants to pay a portion if they use it too. In fact, you can add ten dollars a month for each tenant to more than cover your costs, although that is not counting your time in dealing with it. With a larger building, I charge tenants $5 per studio and most pay.

Keys. Try to get some master keys (a master key is a key that fits many locks), which only you as landlord will maintain. Tenants will have different locks and keys, but you will have easy emergency access using a master key. For public doors, do not have all the locks keyed alike, because if you need to change one lock you will not have to change all of them. I periodically change the exterior door locks, for example, because after a while, many keys get duplicated by artists and given to friends.

Most important, keep two duplicate keys for each of your locks and your tenants' locks in one place. I buy from Wal-Mart a cubbyhole-type fishing box, to keep all the keys separated. There will be times when you need access and you don't want to spend an hour trying to figure out how to get in.

The prices vary widely for locks. I don't think extra-expensive locks are necessary for interior studio doors. I worry more about the exterior locks to the building. Home Depot has several types, some with attached deadbolts on one key, and they seem the most reasonable. You can find inexpensive standard locks in most chain stores all over the country.

Water Heater. If you need only one water heater, then buy it, especially if it is only a replacement for an existing one. If you have several tenants and you need a very large water heater, then it is usually easier to rent one. Either through your utility company or privately (the utility people will tell you where to go if they don't lease), leased water heaters are cheap. The company pays for installation and the fee usually runs about $15 per month. It will take a few years before it becomes a disadvantage, but you can consider it like an easy loan; instead of you putting out the money, they are. On an operational side, if anything goes wrong, they are responsible. Make sure that the heater is installed with a pan under it, if the floor below might be damaged in the event of a leak.

Water and Sewer. If you have leaks, you will pay in water charges. Make sure you don't have running toilets and dripping sinks. The hard part, if you have tenants, is trying to determine whether they are running their water or have drips and are not telling you about them. You have to keep badgering your tenants so they will be responsive. Tell them you will pay to have any and all leaks fixed. The problem becomes having access to their premises and coordinating that with the plumber's schedule.

Telephone. If you switch companies, your old telephone company will call you up and offer you money to get you back. Check all the deals; you shouldn't be paying high long-distance rates anymore. One trick, if you are living in your space, is to try to get a residential phone rather than a commercial line that will cost you a lot more. Guidelines with the phone companies have nothing to do with zoning or building code guidelines. Tell them it's your 'loft' or your hobby space, and try to get the lowest rates. Whether they classify you at a higher rate or not only makes a difference when it's time to pay the bill, not when you pick up the phone.

As was mentioned, it is more efficient to have more than one line, especially since you need one for the Internet, which can also be used for the fax. You will want to represent yourself as a business to suppliers, and all businesses have a different number for fax. Try to have a web address as well.

Insurance. You will need fire and property insurance and a liability policy. The fire and property policy will protect you against fire and other damage to the property – everything from wind damage to a truck hitting the building. Liability will protect you if someone falls and decides to sue you. You should have these policies to protect your assets, and if you have a mortgage the bank will insist upon it.

Liability insurance is based on the use of the property and the square footage; it can also be based on other things, such as annual sales, but that would not usually affect studio use. Office space has one of the lowest ratings, and believe it or not, an artist's studio is not much above it. So don't emphasize industrial equipment; reinforce the image of someone painting on a canvas on an easel for the brokers. Having rentals will affect the rate, however.

Fire and property insurance is based on the value of the building, especially the replacement cost, as well as on the amount of coverage you want. Other influencing factors can include whether the building is frame or brick, how old, what condition, and whether there is a sprinkler system. Generally, you either will buy a policy for 80% of the replacement cost of the building, or buy a flat policy, which means that if the building burns down you get whatever amount your policy states, regardless of what it takes to rebuild.

The 80% policy might be difficult in a large, old building because the price you paid for the building might be far below the replacement cost.

In a flat policy, the gray area might result if you were to have a substantial fire in more than half of the building, for example, and the insurance paid its maximum to you but it was not enough to rebuild the part that was destroyed. You are then out of luck. While you might have enough to reimburse yourself for your investment, you might not have enough to return the property to its former size and condition.

No matter what you do, if you do not have IBM's resources, you will have to take a chance. I try at least to cover my investment as well equal my estimation of the market value. I cannot cover the replacement cost. I think it is more important to spend part of that money on fire prevention measures.

Even if you understand all the reasons insurance rates go up and down or how rates are calculated, it might not help you much. I have learned that there are two important things you have to do with an old building. Since a lot of insurance is based on square footage, try to minimize the footage. Brag to the banks, but be humble to the IRS, city appraisers and insurance agents. You might also want to downplay the activity. Especially for workers' compensation insurance, an employee doing administrative work has a much lower rate than a maintenance person. You will probably not have people doing separate jobs, so emphasize the lowest-rated tasks.

The other important thing I've learned is to ask the insurance agent why the bill is so high. I tell them I've compared their bills with "my other properties" and something doesn't seem to be in line. They will mumble something and say that they will check other companies and see what they come up with. I can't tell you why this works, but two weeks later, they will call and say they have indeed found a lower rate by switching companies, or doing whatever. I've lowered my rates for one building from $12,000 per year to about $5,000. Try to find a nice broker.

Finally, insurance rates keep going up. In many instances, companies raise the value of your property and so increase your coverage, which of course increases your premium. Even during recession years when all property values were going down, including the insurance companies' own properties, they would claim a higher value for their customers' properties. You want sufficient coverage to compensate you in case of a total loss (value minus land value, which stays regardless of what is on it), but you might want to watch how quickly they raise your appraisal, because it might not be realistic.

Insurance for your personal property is another matter. You can get insurance to cover your equipment, but your "equipment" might not be worth covering unless you have some expensive, individual pieces of value such as a table saw, kilns, and so forth.

Artwork is another matter. The bottom line for struggling artists is that, even though someone else might pay several thousand dollars for your artwork and then pay extra for an insurance policy that will cover this sale, your million- dollar collection of your own work cannot be insured because you won't be able to afford the policy. You might be able to take out a homeowner's policy, which is cheap and can cover some of your art that is not used for business, but it will be very limited. Instead, take what money you can and invest it into a good fire and security system. Also, spend a little time in covering up your work with plastic. You will be surprised how much water and dust can get to your work in an industrial building.

Taxes. Real-estate taxes go up because cities need more money and they encourage appraisers to find appreciation. Even during recessions, bills go up. If your bill goes up, appeal. It is a very simple thing to do. Fill out the one-page appeal form, and also make sure you request a hearing in person. Then appear and tell them how old the building is, that it's being used by artists because no one else wanted it, that you are barely getting by, that no structural improvements have been made, and so forth. You will win. If you do this by written appeal alone, you won't. They won't understand a thing you are talking about when you talk about art, but it works. Tell a sob story.

Snow Removal. Before you sign leases with tenants, think about who will shovel snow from the front door and steps. I try to set it up so that tenants can help. I supply shovels and deicer, but I don't promise high-class office building services.

For artists who might own studio buildings in cold climates, have it in your leases that tenants pay a certain fee (I usually charge $5 to $10) every time the truck comes to plow the snow. This way the plow's per-visit charge is covered. I have to send out bills about twice during the season, but the system works.

Maintenance. Find a person to regularly clean the public areas. Only a regular worker will know the quirks of the building, and you don't have time to keep training new people.

You can use a cleaning service that will charge you triple what you pay an individual. Of course, if you hire someone yourself, you need to be set up for payroll. You can barter with a tenant, but that might backfire if you aren't satisfied with his/her work. The advantage of using a tenant, of course, is that you have someone in-house who is trusted by everyone, and if you go out of town, then that person can help watch everything.

You can divide up the maintenance expense among your tenants and include this fee in their leases.

Supplies. There are many distributors and janitorial supply houses. I suggest you simply stop by a Wal-Mart or equivalent three or four times a year and buy the cheapest toilet tissue you can find by the box - 24 four-packs to the box (or the largest packages they carry). If you are using paper towels, the same thing is true. The janitorial supply stores seem to charge a lot more. Check around for prices, then buy light bulbs by the box.

The major question is, where will you store these supplies so as not have your tenants dipping into them? Get a locked closet, and make sure only authorized people have access.

Just like having emergency supplies and equipment, you might as well try to stock as many of the regular supplies as possible.

Wear Two Hats. The tough part of being an artist and landlord in your building is that your artist tenants are probably friends and colleagues as well. They may either resent you because they are paying you rent or because when they have a problem, you might not clear it up immediately.

Keep in mind that a problem could be something that you should repair, something they just want and think you should provide and pay for, or something that is obviously their fault, like not having money to pay you the rent. In all cases, fault, blame and responsibility will be transferred to you regardless of logic.

This tendency can hurt your operations unless you take a few steps to minimize it. First of all, you should have established a business entity to which they pay rent. You can even have the mailing address be somewhere other than to your address or to a post office box, but then it's difficult for tenants to simply hand you their rent checks. You must decide who will call if a tenant's rent gets behind. In most instances, it will be you, because you can't afford to hire someone else and you can't afford to not be tough. Only you know how important it is to get all the rents collected in order to pay your bills.

From the beginning, establish the rules regarding the rental. While you don't have to plead poverty, say up front that they are in an arts building and that it only holds together if all artists pay and contribute to the environment. Tell them verbally, so you are used to talking to each tenant regarding this subject (even though it is in the lease, it doesn't come alive until you verbalize it). Tell each tenant that if he/she does not pay, it will jeopardize the entire building and you will take immediate action. You will separate friendship from business. They are renting the studios with that understanding.

Try not to be taken advantage of. Perhaps I'm too nice, but if I had a dime for every "Oh, Eric, could you help me for a minute" I've heard, I'd be well off. Because I am the lessor, tenants sometimes think I am also the maintenance person (as I once was) who is available at a moment's notice to help in their studios. Never mind getting them to help you! You will find your own line, but I finally stated that I would only do manual labor and risk hurting my back for my own work; I won't do it for others. I also indicated in memos periodically who (someone in the neighborhood or the maintenance person) was available to help and for how much an hour – and then gave phone numbers. I stated to the tenants that if they needed fifteen minutes' help, they would have to pay for a minimum of one hour (about eight to ten dollars). I told them to make their own arrangements. It got me off the hook and it worked. And ten dollars did not seem like a lot. Usually there are local people who would love to get this kind of extra cash work, and usually one hour becomes two or three.

An odd aspect of renting to people you know, or will know, is that you learn things about them that you might not really want to know. It could be financial; it could be their housekeeping habits. I was involved with a few repairs and couldn't believe how dirty some fairly sophisticated artists were. And when I say dirty, I mean as in not washing their bathtub in two years. It just goes with the territory.

You'd better have a thick skin. You need to be mentally resistant. Keep in mind your own artistic ambitions. Over the years, I've found that the more professional artists understand your needs. The ones who don't usually won't meet your standards anyway.

Legal. You can learn the hard way, as I did, but tenants who get behind in most cases never get caught up. Be nice if someone comes to you and volunteers that a rental payment will be a week late. As for the tenants who don't bother to talk to you until you call to ask why the payment has not been given, don't expect them to change. It will only get worse. I also tell tenants that their "late fees" don't even cover the interest my bank charges me when, as a result of their non-payment, I need to then borrow to pay the building's expenses. Of course, I don't have to tell them anything, but I've found that many artists have absolutely no concept of what the owner might be faced with.

Find a lawyer who specializes in landlord-tenant cases; there are some who are in landlord/tenant court every week with two hundred cases. That person or firm will be all set up. When someone hasn't paid as promised (I always give one chance) or hasn't addressed the issue with you, assume that it will only get worse. First give the tenant a notice, if called for in the lease. Then contact the lawyer and get eviction proceedings started. Almost all tenants find the money somehow.

Your personal lawyer is not the person to handle this. These cases are a dime a dozen, but the trick is to get them handled quickly. Use people that can do the proper paperwork in their sleep. It will make a big difference.

Accounting. Get a computer program such as Quicken or QuickBooks and enter all your deposits and checks. Give each category a name. My basic expense categories are for mortgage payment, electricity, gas, insurance, labor, supplies, taxes, trash, water and sewer, telephone and office. Everyone will tell you different categories, and I'm sure your accountant will suggest those which fit his/her system. At the very least, however, the ones I've just listed will serve to give you a good idea where your money is going.

Then get a large-format checkbook and write checks for everything. Writing the checks doesn't take very long. If you are really into the Internet, you can get at hardly any cost (one advertised at $8.95 a month) a service that will pay your bills as you direct and mail them to the various companies.

Payroll. I've already mentioned often that the best idea is to set up as a corporation, or some sound legal entity, and to set up a payroll system so that you are not hiring employees illegally. There are so many forms and taxes to file, the best idea is to spend a bit more money to have a payroll service do it all for you. Make sure they are responsible for all filings. They will do federal and state and all year-end W2s and reports. After doing it both ways, I simply don't think it's worth your energy, especially since you are not aware of all the future regulation changes. These outfits will handle your account no matter what your size or how often you write payroll checks, except that the fee will be a bit higher on a per-check basis. During winter months, I only use this service every two months; during summer, usually every other week. Your only other option is to use a software program like QuickBooks, but you will need to update it every year.

Energy Programs. Take advantage of the various energy-saving programs. Accept the free survey offers. The utility-paid inspectors will draw up recommendations and present a program to replace light fixtures, ballasts and bulbs, and make various insulation proposals. You will save money, because all the bulbs will be replaced at a cost lower than you would pay for replacing just the ones that go out.

The gas or oil companies may offer you similar proposals. There will be a time when some piece of equipment, such as the main boiler, gets to the point where you have to decide whether to patch it once more or to bite the bullet and install a new one. If you wait and also inquire periodically, because these programs seem to come and go depending on government funding, you may be able to synchronize a replacement during one of the programs at a substantial discount.

Collecting Rent. Few landlords 'bill' tenants, because after signing a lease they are expected to pay by the first of the month. If payment is later than ten days (normally, but it could also be five days), a late-charge notice is sent to the tenant.

Unless I am sure to be around to ask for rent in person, I send monthly bills to all tenants. With computers, it really is easy to generate an invoice, which I do and send at least two weeks before the first of the month. When the invoices are prepared, a late charge is added if anyone has not paid the current rent. With twenty-five artists in one building, there will always be about five who are behind. Each month, there will be a couple of others who owe differing amounts because of arrangements made regarding their seasonal use of utilities, rent increases, or other fees. Also, each month, I usually have something to communicate - problems with the building or things such as trying to encourage tenants to keep their trash in sealed bags, or not to use the freight elevator for convenience, and so on.

Copies of these invoices are stapled together and I use them during the month to record payments. I also go through these once and make necessary calls to whomever is behind.

It sounds like a lot, but in practice it takes about one hour once a month to generate the invoices and mail them. I know it encourages payments, because there is a standard reminder on the notice that late fees will be added after the tenth of the month.

I am sure there are countless computer programs to keep track of accounts receivable and prepare invoices. No matter what system you use, I think it helps to remind the tenants. After all, to keep it an arts building, you must rent to artists, and artists do not have a good track record for organization. Monthly bills might be the easiest way to remind them.

Taking Credit. Some landlords are beginning to take rent by credit card. If you want to be able to accept credit cards, do not use a distributor or agent. Do it through the bank. Most agents charge a monthly fee plus a monthly rental for the equipment. Unless you are doing a lot of other business, you don't need this. We do it by telephone and the entire fee is just $5 per month plus, of course, a percentage of each charge.

Frankly, I don't think it pays to allow tenants to pay their rent by credit card. Good tenants will give you checks on time; bad tenants will charge to buy themselves a bit more time, but soon they will reach their credit limit, and you will be back where you were, except out about 3%.

On a thousand-dollar rent payment, that's giving up $30. Good tenants may want to charge so they can get mileage credit, but why give away 3% of your money just so they can take a trip?

Preventing Crime. If you take a few steps, you can prevent bad things from happening. This will keep your expenses lower. Sloppiness in this area can cost you hundreds if not thousands of dollars. If you allow situations where crime occurs, you will not only have to deal with possible physical damage to your building (and remember, you have a deductible in your insurance policy), but you will lose tenants who will not want to rent in an unsafe building.

Always rent to straightforward artists; avoid rentals to questionable artists. In this day and age, many people are buying drugs, using drugs and dealing drugs. If this activity begins in your building, it is a sure path to disaster. Even if you don't know what takes place in private studios, you can begin to detect drug activity by noticing what types of "visitors" are coming into the building.

It has all come together at this point - spacious floors, exposed brick, high ceilings, good heat, work sink and great light - plus time to do creative work. A great studio is the result of all the effort taken to make the building work. It will last for many years into the future. (Artist Betsy Damos)

As was mentioned in the Construction chapter, you can hire locals to help shovel snow or sweep outside. Don't let the neighborhood know what kinds of valuables (tools, computers, TVs) you have inside, because the word will spread. But being friendly and making friends might help get your property on a 'don't touch' list. Unless of course, the neighborhood drug participants get inside.

If a streetlight or exterior light goes out, get it fixed that day. If someone urinates outdoors or leaves trash, get it taken care of that day. Even one day of neglect will allow more to happen. I've seen entire blocks change in a matter of weeks, and I've noticed the progression. I am convinced that if the first case of negligence had been corrected, in each case the negative result would not have occurred.

On an operational basis, develop a system and have the help to make sure that all small problems are attended to immediately. This will also carry over to tenants' needs. It will save you a lot of money whether you realize it or not.

CHAPTER 10
Loft Living
as an Accessory Use

*Some bedrooms in studio/lofts are located behind hidden
doors, just in case an inspector or landlord should walk in.*

Living in your studio is a desire and a concern. Not
only are there internal considerations, such as exposure to
odors, but it is also the most difficult thing to do in most
communities where there are strict building and zoning
codes.

Size. In some cities where loft laws have allowed
residential living as an accessory use, the residency
portion of the space cannot be more than 20%. Of course
this is all nonsense, because no one can really say where
the workspace ends and the living space begins.

A bedroom can be a permanent space or just a
couch that converts to a bed. Kitchens are used in
commercial settings so that employees can heat up their
lunches. A living-room couch is the same as a waiting-
room couch. A dining-room table doubles as a conference-
room table.

You really can't distinguish between the two types
of activities. And since these components make the studio
more attractive anyway, why not save the money of an
apartment and live there as well?

Of course you need to determine if living in your
studio is compatible with your lifestyle and with the lifestyle of your family. What is appropriate for a single artist
might not be appropriate for an artist with young children.

Once you have determined that you want to live in
your studio, the only real reason that you may not be able
to would be that the zoning will not allow you to have your
commercial space as your permanent residential address.
That is not to say that 99% of artists won't try to do so in
any case.

Children. A word about family concerns. Many readers might not have dependents, but many will have in the future. If you are thinking long-term, you will want to think about whether a studio is an appropriate space to raise children. I think it is, but not without careful thinking about safety. First, while you might not be licking the floor, a small child might. There are issues of lead paint and other toxic materials left over from previous days. There are issues of your materials and equipment. You don't want a small child accidentally turning on a table saw. The same way that guns should not be kept in the same home with children, less obvious things can become just as lethal.

There will be other issues, such as their friends coming over to play, school buses picking them up in an industrial neighborhood, or outside play opportunities. In New York City, no one will blink an eye; in a small town, other children will snicker when your son or daughter comes out of a factory to go to school.

Studio/loft combos are desired not only to save money, but also to be closer to the work. You will need to consider whether having a spouse and children so near will end up interfering with, rather than helping, your work.

A creative studio can be a wonderful environment for a family, but it can also become more of a conflict than it is worth.

Location. Wonderful old buildings are charming. They are less charming when you are afraid to walk around the block. They become a nuisance when you need to run to the grocery store, but you can't get there easily because there are no grocery stores catering to the industrial neighborhood.   Then there are a host of nighttime worries.

People choose homes in neighborhoods for basic reasons – convenience to jobs, shopping, schools and recreation. They also choose safe neighborhoods, if they can afford them. You might have the best liberal intentions, but you need to think really hard before you send your child to an inner-city public school.

Artists generally don't need to worry as much about

safety, only because they are not driving a brand-new Lexus or Mercedes and not walking down the sidewalk in business suits. But this doesn't mean that crime doesn't exist.

I used to comment that in a poor neighborhood in Washington, D.C., stranger-to-stranger crime was low, because many of the criminals went to the better sections of town to mug tourists and came back to our neighborhood to sleep. But drug crime was rampant, and I had one tenant whose hobby was to chart all the killings within a one-mile radius of the studio building. Another tenant counted 400 gunshots one night. Amazingly, no one was killed that night.

I know people who have been victimized in the best of neighborhoods. Our studio building has had only minor disturbances over a twenty-plus-year history, knock on wood, but you cannot live in a city in this county today without giving location – and the related security issues – a lot of thought.

Kitchen. Take a creative approach; most artists I know have minimal kitchens. If they are lucky enough to have sinks, they have it made. With a refrigerator, a microwave, and a small propane or electric burner set, a full kitchen is made.

Cabinets can be metal shelving left over in the building, old wood cabinets from the dumpster that can be painted creatively, or any range of plastic boxes attached to walls or screwed under counters.

Counters can be anything from preformed counters bought at the lumberyard to urethane-coated old doors and plywood. Refrigerators can be bought secondhand; try covering them with silver paint.

The point is that function comes first. You have an art studio; you are not impressing your neighbor with a kitchen out of <u>House & Garden</u>. Going upscale is easy if you can and want to, but it's not necessary. Appliances are throw-away cheap, and it only takes some creative efforts to bring it all together.

I would put a smoke alarm nearby. While it is a bit of a nuisance when the alarm goes off, in my experience, it is always better to know when the toast is burning than not.

Kitchen area of a loft. Notice the wood-built stairs, exposed round duct, and plants. The counter is made of concrete.

Bedroom. Beds in lofts can be put in a variety of places. The traditional space-saving solution in a high-ceilinged studio is to build a loft, which is basically a platform above head height. The mattress goes on top, and the space below can be used for the bathroom, kitchen, closet, office or whatever.

Since bedrooms are normally used at night, I've seen many bedrooms located in interior spaces, without windows. Windows are more important for making artwork.

In many cases, the mattress can be put on the floor, or a plywood platform can be built. Most artists I know find beds from a variety of free sources.

Old buildings can offer an array of possibilities. Realistically, some bedrooms in studio/lofts are also located behind hidden doors just in case an inspector or landlord should walk in. Hopefully, you will find a studio where legally living there won't be an issue.

Guest Room. This might sound too upscale, but do expect visitors. Find an extra space where a bed – even an inflatable mattress – can be put for visiting friends. It's a small thing to fit in but will be handy down the line.

Before and after photos of the living area of a loft. Plenty of natural light, exposed brick, sandblasted ceilings, and simple lighting system. The sprinkler system has been painted brown to blend in with the ceiling.

Living/Dining Area. Living spaces can be anywhere in a studio, as long as you don't have to deal with odors and dust. In the most bizarre industrial setting, you could put down a ten-by-ten foot floor, set up a couch and two chairs, and, aesthetically, most people would be blown away. The contrast of normal living components within an industrial or creative setting is really an automatic design win. Put a tent or light system above, float a wall partition, add a big industrial 'vase' for flowers, and you will be smiling as you sit and look around at your artwork in progress. A table surface mounted on top of almost any type of industrial artifact doubles as your eating table.

Go look at various design books, magazines and fancy displays. In artwork, I never copy; in design, I'm not afraid to pick up an idea and find a cheap way of doing it.

For example, in an exhibition at MASS MoCA, gray-painted 4 by 12-foot, inch-thick plywood platforms were hung from the ceiling with threaded bolt, rather than installed on top of table legs or bases. The 'floating' platform would make a great dining room or conference table. Someday, I might use this idea.

Bathroom. A bathroom sink can be your only sink. You will have to share it with your brushes and anything else that has to be cleaned. If you are lucky, you might have a bathroom sink for non-studio use, with a utility sink for studio use on the other side of the wall.

Wherever you have a drain and vent pipe and can put in a toilet (which demands a four-inch drain pipe) is the best location for your bathroom. A bathroom consists of four walls; approximately 4 x 8 feet is sufficient. A bit larger is nicer but not necessary. If you have tons of space, go for it. Our current bathroom and closet are bigger than any previous living room we ever had. When using sheetrock in a bathroom, make sure you use 'greenboard' which can take moisture, unlike normal sheetrock.

Depending on whether they are inspected or not, often showers and toilets are set on top of platforms to allow for the trap to be on the inside of the studio and not in someone else's space below. With high ceilings, we built our entire bathroom on a two-foot-high platform, allowing all the pipes to pass under the new floor. A sink can be almost anything that holds water and has a hole for a drain. Metal bowls, plastic bowls, glass bowls or, of course, regular sinks can be used and customized. Showers also can have a variety of bottoms that direct water into a drain; functional water supply can be as simple as a garden hose.

If you have a high ceiling, you could simply build the four walls about eight feet high and let it remain open at the top. If you add a ceiling in order to be able to use the space above, you will need to exhaust the moisture. Frankly, not according to code, I've left a vent into the larger space using a vent cap, since going through the roof would have been a problem. Normally, code requires you to vent moisture to the outside.

Make sure you use GFI electrical outlets in the bathroom (as well as in the kitchen area) to prevent electric shock.

A bathroom can be as formal or informal as you want. If you want to sneak it in, you can justify it, because many manufacturers have full bathrooms for their employees to shower and change in after doing messy work, as well as having emergency wash systems in case any chemical gets splashed in their eyes or on their bodies.

Separation from Work Space. For most artists, it seems natural to have one big open space. Why get away from your work? But in actuality, after a while you do need some separation. It can even be healthy not to see something you are working on for a while, and then to take a fresh look at it later. You might be depressed with how the work is coming and just need to get away for a while. If you are living in your studio, you don't have the option to leave for home. So some physical separation wall or device might be a good thing to design into your space.

Furniture. As with everything else, your studio decoration will not be comparable to a traditional residence. Go with the character of the building. If it's a former theater, do something with theater seats; if you have a gas station, put your living room or garden in the car pit; if you have a bowling alley, keep a lane or two for your own private games; if you have a former manufacturing facility, keep some of the old signs and employee artifacts and frame them; if you have a motel, keep the furnishings to reflect the former use.

You don't need a traditional couch when odds and ends will be more fitting and cheaper. Old office chairs are now in fashion. You don't need a traditional dining table when any surface sheet on top of any type of base will do.

You might be poor, but you are rich in art. You probably have an art collection of your own work that few millionaires could afford (at retail). This is you chance to display it. It helps that large canvases, for example, cover up old walls and holes.

Aesthetically, anything goes inside an industrial space. One artist had a coffin for a coffee table; another couldn't cope with the walls and ceiling, so he erected a tent and you felt like you were in the desert; another found a solution to a bad floor and filled it with river stone - why not a sandy beach while you are at it? I've seen large round stones placed over a drain, and with the water hookup above it seemed like a Japanese shower; a former dentist's chair from a WWII era office building turned arts building became the featured chair in one loft. Many other lofts have sports and games added - basketball hoops, skating floors, darts, bocce, and tennis, to mention just a few.

Large tropical plants seem so out of place in an industrial building that they are the perfect ingredients to soften the edges of your loft. You probably have enough room to add a Tarzan rope to the mix. Use your imagination and don't take it seriously.

Enjoyment. When it's all said and done, why not get some enjoyment out of your loft? Obviously, the main satisfaction comes from having superb studio space that will include functional spaces for all aspects of your work. Gone should be the days when everything has to be cleared away in order to begin each new project. A good studio will have several projects in development simultaneously.

But when you leave your studio and commute the fifty feet to your living area, you might want to include some fun gimmicks. For example, I had extra upstairs space. Rather than just put a few chairs on the floor, and since the existing floor had such a slope to it, we poured a concrete patio (poured inside leveled squares that were formed by a 2x4 grid). Outside the concrete area, we installed basic commercial carpet. But in the carpet area, we drilled five large holes about four inches deep. Add a putter and some golf balls, and we can now putt on our very own putting green. I didn't do it because I'm a golfer; I'm not. It was just a fun thing to add.

Try to give yourself at least one luxury: something that you will use or see everyday. Maybe it's a special design for your shower, or for your bedroom, or for your kitchen, but if you spend just a little bit extra, you might have a smile on your face every day. A successful studio/loft is something to be proud of.

This 14-unit building serves as temporary housing for artists and has galleries on the street-level floor. It is just two blocks from MASS MoCA.

Alternative. When residential use is simply not going to happen because of zoning and building codes, you might have to look around for alternative solutions. In many communities, you will find industrial buildings mixed in with residential neighborhoods. You might be able to buy a house and a building within a few feet of each other. By dividing up the house, you can package a studio and residential space together. Since the studio is the primary focus, the residential space need not be as large or 'normal' as it would be if it were the only property.

In North Adams, a fourteen-unit apartment building just two blocks from MASS MoCA, also containing five small stores, was offered to me for just $30,000. The apartments were too tiny for year-round or normal living, but combined with a studio in the mill, or used for a few months by artists working at one of the art centers, it became a perfect package. Rather than trying to renovate the building by ripping out all the broken-up spaces and plumbing, we went 'with the flow' and kept the tiny apartments intact.

CHAPTER 11
Artists' Buildings
& Organizations

There may be some very good artists working in the building, but there certainly will be a share of not-so-good artists.

In your search for space, you will come across large buildings – larger than you ever dreamed. From thinking about personal studios to thinking about renting out to others in order to reduce your expenses, your mind will also run into doing other ambitious projects. You might establish an artists' organization, or simply bring like-minded colleagues together. A building full of creators has both potential and pitfalls.

In addition to accidentally getting yourself mixed up with a larger endeavor, you might be already representing an organization that needs new quarters. No matter for what reason, the larger the building complex, the more impact you can have on the art scene of your community, but at the same time, the more complications can develop.

Artists' Committees. In most condominiums (and cooperatives work the same way), a committee is formed to run the affairs of the complex, under the rules of the bylaws. If you've ever worked with a group, you know how complex each issue can become and how difficult it is to find a resolution. Obviously, there are advantages to group action and commitment of others. They will care about the building and become watchers; they will help get good tenants and make sure other tenants don't get out of hand. They will divide up the work to do special events and projects. But committees by definition take power away from an individual authority. If you own your building, and you rent to other artists, then you can decide to do whatever you want without seeking majority consensus. Obviously, it helps to be a diplomat if, for example, you are deciding on a new wall color for the hallway. But in the end, single owners get things done more efficiently.

When circumstances call for a group building, then try to wrestle with it as best as you can. Focus on the positive elements and make a schedule so that issues are decided upon without getting too drawn out. Go over the bylaws carefully and make sure they are followed. The best result of an artists' committee is that the group can become a force to make positive change in the larger community.

Artists' committee meeting in one of the loft studios. Many issues can be resolved this way, and a sense of community is maintained.

Screening Candidates. Even in a building that is individually controlled, I sometimes want committees to form. For example, in my first warehouse turned studio complex, which I still own, the fact that I live in another state means that I can't be there. I encouraged an artists' committee to form to help screen new tenants. While it could cost me money if a vacant studio stays unoccupied longer than normal, the group more than makes up for any delay by knowing and attracting new prospective tenants and by making sure quality artists are chosen. If the building lost its artistic atmosphere, it would become a much less attractive place to rent.

Open Studios. With a group of artists in one building, a lot of energy and art activity is generated. Artists like to exhibit, and often artists want to show their studios to the public through 'open studios.'

These are "Open Studio" brochures, designed by resident artists for studio buildings in Washington D.C. Many of the brochures include a brief history of each building, a map of the studios and/or directions to the building and a brief write-up on each of the participating artists.

With a large enough group, which can be made larger by coordinating open studios with other artists' buildings, a good number of visitors will be attracted. Often strong sales will occur because collectors like to see and buy artwork before it gets into a gallery. An open studio day can really be an enjoyable event. With a lot of artists all chipping in to cover expenses, each contribution can remain minimal and the work can be divided up. You will think up many types of joint events geared for the creators in your building.

Invited Curators and Collectors. Often curators want to go to artists' buildings because they can see several artists during one trip. They can also be invited to come during open studios or for private visits. The only downside can occur when one artist invites a curator who might take greater interest in a neighbor's work.

One time I invited a collector who was interested in one of my pieces, but by the time she left the building (you can see I was being too nice), after I had introduced her to a couple of fellow artists in the building, she chose one of their works and I lost a sale.

In one artists' building, there were periodic lectures, visits and activities going on. Nothing was formally organized, but having a critical mass of artists in one place allowed for some interesting events.

Parties. Life in an artists' building can be interesting. Because low-cost buildings are usually found in bad neighborhoods, often artists feel locked in and isolated. Although the best artists' buildings have private - rather then communal - studios, the advantages of several artists being in the same place is the opportunity for interaction. Sometimes casual meetings take place in the hall, sometimes two or three artists share a beer in a studio, and once in a while something is half- planned so that more artists know about it and can attend a get-together. Although it sounds a bit unprofessional, get-togethers actually make the immediate environment a bit more interesting. In one building that also had an art gallery, regular openings livened up the scene. The only downside is the necessity and responsibility for cleaning afterwards.

Security and Fire. The bad thing about other artists being nearby is that you don't know if they have safe or unsafe habits. If they accumulate trash, smoke, leave materials in the open rather than in metal cabinets, or are careless about locking doors and turning off lights, the least harm will be that your share of the expenses will go up; the worst case would be that your work and property would go up in smoke. Younger tenants, in particular, don't seem to have the same 'preventive' mindset that experience brings. It only takes one incident of the fire department coming to a smoke-filled floor in the middle of the night and finding wax in a pot on a small burner left on after the artist had gone for the day, to sober you up about your tenants' habits and sense of responsibility.

On the other hand, you can't be there all the time, and it is sometimes a good thing to have someone else there. If smoke occurs, someone else may smell it in time. Keep fire extinguishers in the public halls and require tenants to have their own.

Extra Help. There is always a moment when you need an extra hand. I used to think that I really only wanted help when my studio needed major cleaning, but on a regular basis, I need only about one hour a week. The trouble was that I needed that one hour in five-minute installments during the seven days. For example, when moving a large, eighteen-foot-wide canvas, I might need someone just for a minute to help hold the other side. When loading up a truck, I might need someone just for those few minutes.

Although there is a limit to how often you can ask for help, your colleagues will have similar needs and will be calling you. If the group or building is large enough, there may be enough money to hire a part-time maintenance person, who also could be a resource for a five-minute 'need help' problem.

Some Positives, Some Negatives. Notwithstanding all the advantages in theory of having colleagues nearby, there is one overriding negative issue that stands out. In most of the planned artists' buildings I know about, the quality level of the group is not high and the atmosphere of the buildings seems 'canned.'

It's hard to describe. There might be some very good artists working in the building, but there certainly will be a share of not-so-good artists. In my estimation, this often happens because the spaces of planned artists' buildings are finished, so that there is little that has to be done by the artist-tenants. This encourages artists who do not like to take risks. In addition, usually there are many costs involved with the result that rents are not really so cheap. This invites affluent artists who might be able to pay, but who might not have the qualifications to get a space if competition was stiffer.

This statement does not mean that all serious artists avoid group buildings, but amateur artists who have the money to rent nice studios often like to be with other artists for support. This is just one step away from 'yuppies' moving in and turning the studio spaces into comfortable condos. For some artists, renting a studio near others is a cheaper way to go than to be back in school paying for instruction. It is just one reason why a group building will have such a mixed bag of artists. If you want to fill your building with serious artists, you will have to work at it.

Buildings that are larger, rougher and with fewer conveniences will attract ambitious artists who need space, and will discourage non-artists. If you are planning a building, keep this in mind.

When I converted my warehouse building in Washington D.C., it was easier to sand all the floors in the beginning, so the studios were a cross between being functional and being beautiful. But the neighborhood still had an 'edge' to it, and I was there to assure that serious artists would become tenants.

A large complex in Miami Beach works because it is privately funded and artists need to apply to get space, which is very affordable to begin with. Artists get almost free studios but are required to be in their studios at least thirty hours a week, give a percentage of their sales to the governing organization, and make themselves available to visitors a few times a week. Artists have no problems with this because the visitors buy a lot of art. The building is in a great neighborhood and accessible to tourists.

Another building was renovated across the river

from Washington, D.C., in Alexandria, Virginia. Initially sought for idealistic reasons, it soon became heavily visited, and artists specializing in crafts took over. The organization set it up so that all studios had windows where tourists could peek in and watch the artists at work. The complex still draws more tourists than any other attraction in the city. It has helped people who do crafts and want to sell their wares directly. The building is not cheap, by any standards, nor is it considered a serious art building anymore. If you are looking to do a building with a tourist hat on, then that might be fine; if you are looking to do a serious art space, then watch out for having it turn out this way.

Many buildings do have idealistic intentions in the beginning, but visit them ten years later and you will see the gentrification of the building, just the way SoHo filled up with eateries and boutiques. Prices will inflate and serious artists will once again be locked out financially.

If you are the landlord, however, you might eventually not care, because you are principally worried about paying bills. You might prefer to lease to various types of tenants. Running a property as a business is fine, if you can make a living. Raising rents may be in your self-interest. If there is adequate demand for commercial, non-artist tenants, then your rent payments might even be more consistent. However, make sure you are prepared to lose the artistic atmosphere of a building, because it will be hard to get it back if you change your mind. Also, make sure that you, as an artist, do not need this type of atmosphere, especially if you still have your own studio and are still working in the building yourself. It is a natural tendency when a unit becomes vacant to rent to the first, economically stable prospect that comes around. If the new tenant does not fit in, you will hear about it from others.

Theater Groups. Studio space for performance, whether for rehearsal or in front of audiences, offers a host of possibilities. Spaces could be made available for both small and large rehearsals. For example, often just three or four actors need to get together to do a reading. Elsewhere on the main stage, a rehearsal could be going on. In another part of the building, someone could be working on costumes or set design, and so forth.

Often groups try to rent or construct one stage. I would recommend a much larger complex where non-traditional stages could be constructed and then moved about. It is important that the space be as flexible as possible to allow for undefined future work. Keep the other arts in mind as you decide upon, and then design, performance space. I believe the future will bring many more cooperative efforts by artists in various mediums.

Residency Facilities. Some studio complexes have studios geared for short-term rentals. This allows artists from all over the world to come and interact, which in turn can benefit the artists who have permanent studios. A legally organized not-for-profit could be formed just for this purpose. The organization would be eligible for additional grants and other funding. The obvious example is the Contemporary Artists Center which we founded, whose primary purpose is to allow visiting artists to use an abundance of studio space.

Even the permanent studios could be rented under the umbrella of a not-for-profit. I am not suggesting you go through this extra administrative and legal work just for fun, because the same activities can be done privately. But if you have a strong volunteer group, it might be possible to get significant funding not only to subsidize the studios, but also to enhance the facility with additional programs.

Privately shared facilities can be done in a variety of ways. One idea I had involved purchasing a farm with several outbuildings and cottages. While you would need to be a millionaire to buy and maintain a property like this, and you would have to spend a lot of time as well, eight or more artists pooling their resources could buy it and hire a caretaker couple to live there. The idea was for food to be served in a common dining room, but there would be separate sleeping cottages. Art studios would be divided up in the barns and outbuildings.

Another time, to celebrate the tenth anniversary of my Washington building, we not only had a celebration, but one small studio was offered to a young artist for six months for free. While I lost some rent, it helped to promote the building and gave everyone a good feeling. Other programs of this sort can be geared to any large complex full of artists.

When housing is in conflict with the industrial zoning, consider purchasing a residential property and partnering it with the main studio property. You might find free rooms in nearby houses to accommodate artists working for short terms in an art studio.

Planned Projects. I've either seen in person or have reviewed the financial data for several large artists' studio buildings and residency centers. There are a few elements that stand out.

In Vermont, there is a medium-sized mill converted into a combination of studios, lofts, and public workshop areas for classes and exhibition galleries. It got strong support from the state and local community, which resulted in some grants and low-interest loans. For what I might have spent $150,000, they spent well over $600,000 in renovating the building. What did they get? The state grants required them to redo the elevator, make all spaces handicapped-accessible and bring all areas up to new code standards. This necessitated new fire doors and new emergency systems. The building is great, but the pressure to pay the bills is also great. I don't think the condition of the building brings in any additional rent. Of the money spent for renovation, much of it paid for "prevailing wages" which means that they probably spent 50% more than I would have bidding out to hire private contractors. In some places in the building, I wouldn't have done all the work. I would have made about a third of the space handicapped-accessible and would have left some studios as walk-ups, and rented them for lower rents if necessary. Although it is a worthy goal to make all arts buildings 100% accessible, it is not smart to do it all the first day if it will destroy the future operation of the building. The owners are doing fine, I hear, but I fear that behind the scenes, there must be a lot of pressure each month to pay the bills.

Remember to keep in mind who's in charge. When large projects are formed, the people involved usually are not the artists themselves, but bureaucrats, lawyers, architects, business owners and educators – all people who are used to working in a much more expensive environment. They will think in terms of office-sized spaces for artists, not airport hangers.

I have a much larger arts building, and a much smaller financial headache each month. Over time, my building is getting better and more accessible. The entire first floor, which includes all the exhibition galleries and the café of the Contemporary Artists Center as well as the Dark Ride Project exhibition and ride, is 100% handicapped-accessible. Someday funds will be raised to replace the old elevator, making the building accessible throughout. If I had made all these improvements the first year, the center would not have been able to carry out all the active programs it did over the past decade.

The center was started because I had an excess of extra space. We cleaned out huge studio spaces and concentrated on a few residency rooms, a kitchen and dining area and some recreational space. We asked low fees of artists and invited important museum directors, curators and visiting artists. We operated on a shoestring budget. It worked. Each year, more programs for artists, and many to benefit the immediate community, have been established. Thousands of people have been positively affected by these efforts.

In three large studio buildings I know about elsewhere in the country, economic strains similar to the Vermont project have occurred because of grandiose plans and too much money invested in the transformation for arts use. By the time all is said and done, founders brag about all the art space being offered to artists, when, in fact, it turns out to be very expensive space geared for artists of debatable quality.

There is no way that a planned arts building can be renovated for visual artists using federal, state and local loans, even with the addition of grants, without the spaces having to be divided into smaller units making the monthly rentals high and making them not such a great deal. A lawyer or a bureaucrat may get excited about offering space at $12 per square foot instead of the going 'office' rate of $24 or $48, but I only get excited if rent can be offered at $1 per square foot.

Don't get me wrong. For some projects, especially ones that have a public element, such as theaters and museums, this type of space renovation may be great. But never have I seen a planned, funded building project that offers space to creators at anywhere near what I would regard as a bargain. If any are out there, I can assure you the space is offered on a short-term basis.

I bring this up because some readers might find a building and get excited about expanded options, while other people who want to help do something for the arts might be looking to start such a building. If they research other projects, they might even read great things about them. Why? Because if you were founding an arts space, you would be doing everything you could to make sure the newspapers got the good spin about the project. Your brochure and press releases would mention only great things. And many artists and participants might indeed be happy. My sense is that very few of the artists involved will be breaking new ground, because I think the economics will be suppressing their work.

The main reason this happens is that publicly funded projects dictate that buildings be renovated to a standard that is far above what is necessary to do work. If you are planning a building for public use or need public funds to have it geared for many people, there is no choice. If you are planning to please no one but yourself and a few artists who will rent from you, the standards are completely different. Certainly the standards are lower, as well, but until the government gives more support to the process of creating art, there is little choice but to deal with current economic forces in real estate.

Please take note that this is perhaps a strong, minority opinion. Just keep it in mind. Several times I have found gigantic properties that potentially could be turned into great art space if the government gave me sufficient money. But I know that by the time I went through the process of getting public funds, the cost per square foot would lock artists out. At the same time, if you change the mission to be mostly about exhibition, and then try to plug in some residency and studio spaces as part of your programs, you might be successful because museum spaces can usually earn income that private artists can not.

In fact, MASS MoCA exemplifies that model. Right in the middle of town, a huge complex of mill buildings became vacant, leaving the city with a very high unemployment rate. A suggestion of an arts use brought strong city and then state support. After a fourteen-year effort on a very tight budget, the museum (exhibition galleries and performance space) opened to the public in the summer of 1999. Its success has given new life to the area. The museum uses its operational funds to bring in artists and performers; if it had to depend on rent from art studios, it wouldn't be in business for more than a week. It is renting out space to commercial tenants, however, for $10 per square foot, which may be dirt-cheap in New York City, but is probably double the going rate here.

This used to be junk space: three white walls, a two-hour paint job on the floor and three halogen lights, and it became a great exhibition and event space. It was later improved, but the rather quick fix-up job allowed the space to be used and tested as a public space. (Photographed during a "Sky Art" conference/discussion at the Contemporary Artists Center; artists (l to r) Robert Henriquez, David Zaig, Otto Piene, Elizabeth Goldring, Tal Streeter)

Take all the suggestions for private buildings and try to incorporate programs that stimulate the community, whether just one or two residencies (perhaps for visiting foreign artists), a community workshop, a Saturday morning art class for children, or other arts events. If you have an abundance of space, it need not cost you much. Apply for public funds for just these projects, and not for the real-estate end. You will be better off, and the programs can then expand.

This is an unusual opinion coming from someone encouraging you to buy buildings and to rent to colleagues. I am very aggressive about solving artists' studio needs; I am only hesitant about your thinking you can make the activities of all your tenants as innovative as your own work. I also worry that artists will get too caught up in real-estate development and perhaps too caught up in new programs, supported partially by public funds that are not easy to obtain.

Exhibition Galleries. In order to sell the art, it has to be shown. Artists' buildings are naturals for public galleries, which are either controlled by an artists' committee, shared equally, or run by a hired (paid or not) curator. Seeing works in a nice gallery could be in addition to seeing work in the studios and talking to the artists during open houses and other events. Again, various legal entities could be formed for this purpose. The other advantage of building gallery-type space in your building is that it offers opportunities to do installations and other non-traditional art that may not be alllowed in the normal marketplace. Your building can be about experimental ideas, and not just framed, salable goods for galleries to sell to decorators.

Linkage. As I've already explained in detail, renting or buying a building is cheaper per square foot if you take a lot of footage. This means getting together with others. Whether you formally organize legally or simply divide up the space and each pays a share, there are real advantages over going alone. Group resources gives you real buying power.

Consider variations. If, for example, you are putting together a group of ten artists in Kansas City to take over an industrial building, perhaps you can each add $150 per month to your monthly contributions, and use that money to rent – and share – a studio in New York City. Consider it as a time-share. Each participating artist can have more than one month in the New York City studio; and if it's pretty large, each artist could have a few inches of space in the stacks to store a few works. Schedules could be reserved a year in advance, with changes possible on a voluntary basis.

The point is that artists usually don't look at the big picture. If there are needs, such as getting bulk materials, inviting curators, getting grants for special shows, building special equipment to make available to artists, and so forth, a group of artists has tremendous power to achieve these ends. I don't want to get into processes and career development in talking about studio spaces, but artists should consider enlarging the package of possibilities.

Not-for-Profit Educational Facilities. In addition to getting our personal loft grandfathered in before they changed the zoning laws to prevent residential use in industrial buildings, when we started our art center in the mill, I discovered that educational facilities are not subject to local zoning ordinances, but to state zoning laws. This might be true in your community. Although the residency programs were geared for adult, professional artists, the center was incorporated as a school. As a school, it can allow artists and 'faculty' and 'administration' to live in the mill as part of the school's programs. This does not exempt the 'school' from building codes that deal with safety issues, but it does allow the residential usage to occur. The rationale is that schools often are in areas where there may be commercial or residential surroundings, but they often have dormitories for students and faculty. State law encourages this use, regardless of what the local community has done with its zoning restrictions. You could use this to allow some residential use under an educational format in one part of the complex. The 'school' does not have to own the property; it could just be a tenant.

At the Contemporary Artists Center, we only had residency rooms for seven artists. But by having lots of studio spaces, we were able to find nearby housing for the remaining artists who came. The first summer in 1990 was great because everything was done on a low-budget, low-expectation basis. The more we built in, the more complicated it became, and the more pressure there was to pay for it all.

Just because you get permission or some support, it doesn't mean that you have to be large. Art centers in this country usually have built up to having a paid staff. In the beginning, it was mostly volunteer sweat labor. Don't risk your money or the health of the real estate by getting ahead of yourself.

I bring up these issues, even though the majority of the book is aimed at helping individual artists achieve large studio space on a low budget, because there is a valid, economic reason to create not-for-profit facilities. They can become tenants, paying perhaps a below-market rent, but at the same time using space that otherwise you may not be able to rent privately. The activity of an arts center attracts artists to your building and makes it easier to rent out your private studio units.

The most important reason might be to establish a rationale for settling in one particular community. If you have decided that Manhattan is not affordable, you will start looking around for other areas. Most areas will be dead places, as far as culture is concerned. If you are lucky, you might find a location that offers some culture, some potential down the line but, of course, not the stimulus that New York offers. North Adams, for me, was that type of place. It had valuable culture nearby, but the potential of the new museum proposal was many years away. In addition to helping scores of artists and community residents by starting the Contemporary Artists Center, I brought world-famous museum and gallery directors to North Adams to interact with resident artists. Could I have done this anywhere? Probably not; we were in a place that was attractive. I could invite a museum curator up and say that while he/she was here, a visit to nearby museums, tickets to the theater, or even a rafting trip down the river could be arranged. Certainly we did not have the budget to persuade people to come for the honorarium.

You might be able to do more than you think. You

are not a major museum, and you might not walk into any town and transform it. However, you can probably liven things up considerably, if there are any connections to the arts to begin with. A nearby college, museum, or cultural attraction helps. A recreational attraction also helps. Look around to see what linkages you can establish.

Finally, I want to emphasize that these types of programs do not need to be expensive or complicated. Creating some residency programs for regional, national and international artists really only consists of providing studio space, perhaps exhibition space, and finding some housing in the area. Inviting interesting speakers from within and outside the art world is not that expensive either. Invite interested area residents to join the artists. Not only did I invite many people I knew in the art world, I found it extremely interesting to invite people outside the art world as well. For example, some of our best lectures have been by mathematicians and scientists who spoke to an audience filled with artists. Over time, we added facilities and equipment. This can help your arts building tenants as well. At the Contemporary Artists Center, we built a "Monster Press" with a plate bed of five by ten feet. Not only do artists come from all over to use this press, it is available to local artists, including tenants, as well.

Don't depend on paying your bills with a not-for-profit tenant, but you might be able to spice up the environment considerably and justify your move away from the urban center.

Art can be a popular addition to any community. Pictured above is the author's "Community Sculpture," an annual beach party where eighty thousand pounds of sand is distributed, curb to curb along a downtown street. Hundreds of residents enjoy making creative sand scultpures during a summer afternoon.

Taking Over A Town. A version of the above mentioned activities is not to formally establish a center, but simply to monopolize the culture in a town. As was mentioned early in the book, every artist should take a trip to Marfa, Texas, to see how one artist, albeit with financial help from the DIA Foundation, bought up a good chunk of a remote town. Don Judd wanted an escape from New York City. He also wanted a place to realize ambitious installations for himself and others. It is one of the most important and visonary examples ever known of an independent studio/installation by an artist.

What you might not be able to do by yourself, you might be able to do with just a small group of fellow artists whom you respect. There are remote places that you can afford. If you go to such a place and you do not have a national reputation, and if you are all by yourself, then you will be forgotten about and the isolation may have a negative effect on your work. If you 'take over the town' with six to ten other artists, you will not only make a strong impact, you will be able to intellectually feed off each other. Something that would be lost in the crowd in the big city might thrive and get a lot of attention in a location where there's not much else going on. You could also make history of sorts by establishing non-traditional spaces.

Keep in mind that, just as Judd kept his SoHo studio, a group could also share the rental of a New York studio. What would be of special interest, however, is not only finding affordable space, as we have talked about during the course of this book, but seeking a new level of creation and a new way of experiencing the art.

Dream a little. If the new complex became so exciting and got some financial support, an audience could be specially bused or flown in. All kinds of linkages, whether by Internet or by actual presence, could eventually be added to the mix. And if the art created within this environment were innovative enough, an audience would find its way there, just as people have found their way to Marfa.

You might think about a small, inexpensive town in the way you might think about an empty studio, an empty gallery and even a blank canvas. Hundreds of thousands of feet of space could be developed exclusively for your art. Gradually, more artists could be added to the original group.

Being a big fish in a small pond has its advantages. Usually the drawback is that the ponds are too far away from resources. But group projects can have an impact as well as a resilience of their own. Residencies in visual arts and performance could be part of the programming. The complex could be only a seasonal adventure until sufficient critical mass developed. Small 'teams' of artists could alternate their residency periods. There are many creative possibilities.

Drive across the country and you will discover hundreds of possibilities. Towns that are just one step from becoming ghost towns still have dozens of former granaries, mining buildings, textile mills, cattle barns, agricultural markets, and so forth. Houses and retail stores could be bought up, quietly, for almost pocket change compared to city prices.

I am not proposing vacating the established centers of culture. What I am advocating is the realization of important work versus struggling and not realizing this work due to of the limitations of the city and the art establishment. Imagine a hundred such places being formed and activated around the country. All of them could be linked up to form a powerful expressive voice in this country. In addition, I would bet that a lot of support could be found for these places, as governmental agencies are looking for ways to support culture in 'rural' America. As a young artist today, I would grab an opportunity to create ambitious work, regardless of the audience. The process of creation is much more important than the business of seeking recognition. Many artists will not agree; the attraction of fame via traditional avenues is too great.

Long-Term Ideas. Artists think only about tomorrow, unfortunately. I hope this manual has helped to lengthen your personal time-line.

My suggestion is to sit back, close your eyes, and think much further into the future. The only assumption I ask you to make is that you will not be a superstar whose works are being bought at auction for half a million dollars or more. But by all means assume that you will achieve some degree of recognition, that your works will be in some museums, that you will still sell a portion of your work, and that your name will be of some importance. Now think realistically about all the work you have or will do during this period – including major works as well as preliminary studies, drawings and other smaller efforts. After decades of work, you should have a small warehouse full of art. What will eventually happen to all this work?

Some artists hope that their children can handle it all; others dream that their dealers will be happy to receive truckloads of work to flood the marketplace.

Realistically, it can't happen unless you have such superstardom. There is a debate going on within the art community about how best to deal with all the art created by the hundreds of thousands of 'pretty good artists,' each of whom might have some reputation and history of sales. Whether done by way of a trust, foundation, simple will, business inheritance, family inheritance, or some other legal way to allow your work to be passed down with a minimum of IRS intervention, most artwork is received by someone as physical goods that have to be inventoried and sent off somewhere. The question is, received by whom and sent to whom? Who would want the liability for maintenance, storage and preservation? In reality, most artwork can't be given away. (Estate matters become extremely complicated for creators; there is some argument that artists would be better off operating as corporations; for more information on this issue, check out A Visual Artist's Guide to Estate Planning, based on a conference co-sponsored by The Marie Walsh Sharpe Art Foundation and The Judith Rothschild Foundation.)

Now think about your real estate. The interesting part of owning large buildings is that eventually, if planned correctly, your debt will be paid off and, if you are renting out space to others, your studio space will be free. In fact, by this time, you might be earning a good income as well as enjoying free space.

Collectors buy art and some open their own museums. As an artist, you don't normally think in these terms. But space that not only doesn't cost you anything, but may also be bringing in income, becomes a valuable asset. Upon your death, you won't need this space to work, of course. Perhaps you can begin to formulate a structure for an 'artists' museum' or an 'artists' center.' Perhaps your studio could be opened to the public, with exhibition space added, and with residencies for deserving young artists to use some of the space. Perhaps you can build into this plan a way for someone to catalog your work and to make it available to the public, even on limited terms. Your building need not be that large for this to work.

How to pay for this? If you plan a fifty-year run, you can easily build in an income source to do this. You can also take out an insurance policy now, in case of an early death.

Obviously, you can simply create art and let someone else worry about this someday. Or you can be realistic about the resources that will be available and make some provisions now. If you make a will, your work is a part of your estate. But handing over your estate to someone who is not equipped to deal with it is foolish.

Why go through only half of the planning? Figure out several possibilities. Industrial spaces in some neighborhoods might become very accessible fifty years from now. It's like putting a thousand dollars in the stock market and not looking at it for half a century. It grows. So can your studio complex. A life full of art can live beyond the artist's life. More than a vanity project, a long-term plan can be an alternative to the establishment's methods of choosing which works of art stay and which are destined to be thrown away. A long-term plan can also be a way for an artist to give back and give new opportunities to a new generation of creators.

Public Goals and Artistic Innovations. Artists need to take a public role. Artists shouldn't only work independently without caring how the government supports the arts, how the establishment – commercial galleries and museums – deals with artists. Studio space is essential to making art. If there are opportunities for the local government or establishment to help, push them along. There are lots of artists out there, and they also have votes and a voice.

Support programs that will help, and keep your goals always in mind. You cannot expect bureaucrats to help if you have not spent the time to educate them. I know that a balance has to be maintained between your artistic-professional life, your personal life and your volunteer life, but a lot of time is still available if you schedule it well.

In many cases, there are grants and funding programs out there which simply have to be matched with an appropriate arts program. However, only artists who know the needs of creators will come up with the projects that the bureaucrats can fund. You can't complain if you haven't done your share.

Summary

TAKING STOCK

There's a lot of information that you have just digested. You now have to put it all in perspective. Relax and take stock. Ask yourself where you are now working, what would you like to have, and what are your real needs. Then add a few dreams.

Ask yourself if you really know the real estate in your area. I know that everyone thinks they do, but then I've discovered that they just skip over many opportunities. It is time to take a fresh look.

If you have a studio now, whether it's a part of your home or a separate place, you have either purchased it (probably as part of a home purchase) or more likely you are renting. Therefore, you have some experience already dealing with sales or lease agreements. You also have had either good or bad experiences with landlords, or with being your own maintenance person in charge of the space.

You probably also work with or know several other artists. You certainly know where other people in your field are working. Go there and look around. Ask lots of questions. Find out what people are paying.

Of course, you want to think about whether you are satisfied with the region or city in which you live. Whether you have dreams or not, you probably will stick it out where you are, at least for a while, until a better job or professional offer comes along. That is not to say you have to rule out a gradual shift. As was mentioned earlier, there are ways to have a part-time studio in a location that is more attractive to you.

Like an old car, which will require you either to make repairs or to know where to take it to keep it running, a cheap studio will require lots of construction knowledge. I hope this manual has given you an idea of how to get started. There is no substitute for experience. You need to get your hands dirty to find things out. My main caution is, while you are learning, don't burn through your money too quickly, only to discover later that you could have done things cheaper.

I used to think it was all beyond me. I was trained as a traditional painter, and I never got into construction. What a shock when my work drifted into sculpture! I am not talented that way, but I have discovered that all trades and all mechanical systems have logical components. You, too, can understand it. You do not have to be the tradesperson assembling the plumbing pipes, but you can understand about water lines, drains and vents. It is not that difficult.

Finally, take pride in your profession. Too often, artists are relinquished to a 'sub' category. No one takes creativity seriously; our national government doesn't support art activity the way other countries do; and, psychologically, artists accept poor, humbling conditions.

You can fight that. You can organize with other artists. You can protest that area museums, large commercial concerns, and local governments are not doing enough. You can protest, picket and lobby for their participation in supporting better studio facilities for artists. Just don't hold your breath to wait for others to satisfy your immediate needs.

Good, affordable and permanent studio / loft space is like a blank canvas; it awaits your creative energy. Photo: Caroline Bonnivier

You can make a difference in your life, your career and the state of arts in your community. You can also set up your profession in a manner that carries you for the rest of your life.

Read The Art World Dream: Alternative Strategies for Working Artists and, together with your knowledge about studio spaces, you should be able to jump many steps ahead of where you are now. I hope you have success.

Sample Commercial Lease. Do not use without checking with your attorney and with state codes. Be sure to customize whatever applies to each individual rental.

LEASE AGREEMENT

This lease agreement is made __(date)__ by and between _____ ("Landlord") and _____, personally ("Tenant").

Witnesseth:

1. Description, Term and Option to Renew.

1.1. Landlord does hereby let unto Tenant, and Tenant does hereby hire from Landlord, Warehouse Studio Unit No. ____on the _____ floor, approximately _____ sq. ft. of the property in the ____(state)_____ known by street address as _____. The term of this Lease shall be for a period of one year, commencing on _____ and expiring on _____ (the "Original Term").

1.2. If Tenant is not in default hereunder, Landlord agrees that Tenant shall have the option (the "Extension Option") to extend the term of this Lease for an additional period of one year (the "Extension Period") following the expiration of the Original Term. Tenant shall exercise such option by giving Landlord written notice of exercise not less than three (3) months prior to the expiration of the Original Term. If such option is exercised, the terms of this Lease shall be the same as those which apply during the Original Term, except that the "Monthly Rent" for the Extension Period shall be increased _____%.

1.3. Tenant shall pay a 5% late charge to Landlord on any monthly rent or installment which is not paid or received by Landlord on or before the tenth of the month when due.

2. Base Annual Rent.

2.1. During and for each year of the entire Original Term, Tenant shall pay to Landlord, as the fixed "Based Annual Rent" for the Leased Premises, the sum of _____ dollars ($_____.00) which sum shall be payable in twelve equal monthly installments of _____ Dollars ($_____.00). Each installment of Base Annual Rent shall be due and payable to Landlord in advance on the first day of each month during the term hereof, checks payable to _____, at _____, or at such other address as may be designated by written notice to Tenant pursuant to the terms hereof.

3. Use and Purpose.

The Leased Premises shall be used as a studio and office for art work provided such uses comply with all applicable zoning, building and other laws, rules, ordinances and regulations of all governmental bodies having jurisdiction over all or any part of the Leased Premises (collectively "Governmental Regulations"). The Leased Premises may be used for no other purpose without the prior written consent of the Landlord. Tenant covenants and agrees that it will use and operate the Leased Premises in compliance with all Governmental Regulations. Tenant shall not use the Leased Premises or permit or suffer the same to be used for any disorderly or unlawful purposes. It is recognized, that in the _____(state)_____, it may be possible to live in industrial artists studios, and Landlord agrees to allow Tenant to do so with Tenants' compliance with such Governmental Regulations as may apply to the premises.

4. Assignment and Sub-Letting.

Tenant shall not have the right to assign this Lease or to sublet all or part of the Leased Premises without the prior written consent of the Landlord in each instance obtained.

5. Delivery of Possession.

Landlord shall deliver possession of the Leased Premises to Tenant upon the commencement of the term of this Lease in "as is" condition, with the following appliances - _____.

After delivery, Landlord shall have no obligation with respect to the condition of the Leased Premises except as expressly provided herein with respect to the roof, mechanical systems, foundation, plumbing and exterior walls.

6. Maintenance and Repairs.

Tenant covenants and agrees that it will throughout the term of this Lease, as its cost and expense, keep and maintain the interior of the Leased Premises in good condition and repair, and that it will be responsible for any and all necessary, appropriate or required maintenance and/or repairs (including necessary replacements and including any necessary repair and replacements to kitchen appliances) to the Leased Premises; provided, however, that Landlord covenants and agrees that it will, throughout the term of this Lease (except in instances of the negligence or intentional act of Tenant, its agents or invitees), at its cost and expense, keep and maintain the heating, plumbing and electrical systems, hallways, foundation, roof and exterior walls of the Leased Premises in good condition and repair. Tenant shall, at its cost and expense, comply with all applicable laws, ordinances and regulations affecting the Leased Premises and the conduct of Tenant's business therein. At the expiration or other termination of this Lease, Tenant shall surrender the Leased Premises to Landlord in good condition and repair, normal wear and tear excepted. Normal office-type trash may be put into the dumpster or designated trash area, not to exceed two bags per week. No food may be put with trash. Food waste must be taken out of the building or put down a garbage disposal.

7. Utilities.

Landlord shall be responsible for heat, water, and sewage. Tenant shall be responsible for telephone and all electricity, and shall change the electrical account into Tenant's name and pay directly.

8. Tenant's Fixtures and Equipment.

All alterations, additions to or improvements in or on the Leased Premises made by either Landlord or Tenant (except movable furniture or attached and unattached equipment put in at the expense of Tenant) shall immediately become the property of Landlord and shall remain upon and be surrendered with the Leased Premises as a part thereof at the termination of this Lease, without disturbance, molestation or injury thereto, and without complaint, claim, contest, litigation or delay by Tenant or Tenant's heirs, successors, assigns, agents, guests, licensees, creditors, pledgees, mortgagees or other persons. Tenant agrees to pay to Landlord on demand the amount necessary to repair to Landlord's satisfaction any damage to the Leased Premises caused by the Tenant's placement, attachment or removal of Tenant's property in, to or from the Leased Premises.

9. Liability and Fire and Extended Coverage Insurance.

Landlord shall, throughout the term of this Lease, at its sole cost and expense, maintain in effect general liability insurance insuring Tenant and such mortgagee(s) against injury to persons (including loss of life) and damage to property occurring in, upon or about the Leased Premises, and shall keep the building containing the Leased Premises insured against loss or damage by fire and extended coverage hazards.

10. Damage or Destruction.

10.1 In the event that the Leased Premises are damaged or destroyed as the result of any casualty covered by the fire and extended coverage insurance described in 9, Landlord shall, as soon as reasonably possible, repair, restore and reconstruct the Leased Premises so that upon completion thereof the Leased Premises will be substantially the same as before the occurrence of said damage or destruction. In the event of any such casualty and restoration, Tenant, at its own expense, shall restore its alterations, modifications and improvements, including its leasehold improvements, furnishings, fixtures and equipment as soon as reasonably possible. The Base Annual Rent shall abate following such fire or other casualty in proportion to the portion of the Leased Premises that are not usable by Tenant.

10.2 Notwithstanding the foregoing provisions of 10.1:

10.2(1) if the Leased Premises are damaged or destroyed by casualty covered by insurance during the last six (6) months of term of this Lease, and such damage or destruction amounts to more than one-half (1/2) of the replacement value of the improvements thereon; or

10.2(2) if the Leased Premises are damaged or destroyed at any time during the term of this Lease and the casualty is not covered by the fire and extended coverage insurance being carried by Landlord; then, and in either of such events, Landlord or Tenant shall have the option, to be exercised upon written notice to Landlord or Tenant within sixty (60) days following such fire or other casualty, to elect to terminate this Lease, whereupon this Lease shall terminate as of the date of the giving of such notice to Landlord or Tenant and the parties shall be relieved of any and all liability or obligation thereafter accruing.

11. Condemnation.

11.1. Tenant agrees that if the Leased Premises or any part thereof shall be taken or condemned for public or quasi-public use or purposed by any competent authority, or sold in lieu thereof, Tenant shall have no claim against Landlord and shall have no claim or right to any portion of the money that may be awarded as damages or paid as a result of any such condemnation, taking or purchase; and all rights of Tenant to damages therefore, if any, are hereby assigned by Tenant to Landlord.

11.2 Upon a condemnation or taking of the whole of the Leased Premises, or so much thereof as to make the Leased Premises, in the discretion of Landlord or Tenant, unsuitable for Tenant's continued occupancy for the uses and purposes for which the Leased Premises were leased, or upon a sale in lieu thereof, the term of this Lease shall cease and terminate from the date of such condemnation, taking or sale, and Tenant shall have no claim against Landlord for the value of the unexpired term of this Lease.

11.3 If only a portion of the Leased Premises is condemned, taken or sold and Landlord determines that the remaining Leased Premises are suitable for Tenant's continued use and occupancy as above provided, this Lease shall, only as to the part so condemned, taken or sold, terminate on the date of such condemnation, taking or sale, and the Base Annual Rent shall thereupon be reduced in proportion to the area of the Leased Premises so condemned, taken or sold.

12. Security Deposit.

12.1 Tenant has deposited with Landlord ("Escrow Agent"), upon the execution hereof, the sum of _____ Dollars ($_____.00) (the "Security Deposit"), of which $_____.00 represents the first monthly rent for _____(date)_____ and $_____.00 represents the last monthly installment of the Base Annual Rent due during the Original Term, as a security deposit to be held by the Landlord pursuant to the following terms. If the Tenant fails to occupy the Leased Premises at the commencement of the Original Term, the Security Deposit shall be paid to the Landlord as and for liquidated damages. If the Landlord fails to ready the Demised Premises for occupancy and deliver same pursuant to 5, the Security Deposit shall be returned to the Tenant with no further liability of either party hereunder. Upon the commencement of the Original Term in accordance with the terms of this Lease, the Security Deposit shall be paid to the Landlord to be disposed of as hereinafter provided.

12.2 After payment of the Security Deposit to Landlord pursuant to the foregoing, Landlord shall have the right to avail itself of the Security Deposit to cure any defaults on the part of Tenant or for the performance of any of Tenant's obligations hereunder. Provided no default exists hereunder, any balance of the Security Deposit not used by Landlord to cure Tenant's defaults or perform Tenant's obligations, shall be credited against the last monthly installment of the Base Annual Rent, unless Tenant exercises its right to extend the term of this Lease pursuant to 1.2, in which event such remaining balance shall be credited to the last monthly installment of Base Annual Rent due at the end of the Extension Period.

13. Default.

If (i) any rent or other sum of money required to be paid by Tenant hereunder, or any part thereof, shall not be paid on the day when such payment is due, or (ii) during the term hereof, Tenant shall become bankrupt, make a general assignment for the benefit of creditors, or take the benefit of any insolvency act relating to Tenant's ability to pay its debts, or (iii) there is any default by Tenant in the performance and/or observance of any term, condition, provision or requirement of this Lease (other than in the payment of money) required to be performed and/or observed by Tenant hereunder and such default shall continue for a period of ten (10) days after written notice thereof from Landlord;

then, in any of the events enumerated above, Landlord shall have the right, at its option, by giving written notice to Tenant, to terminate this Lease, and thereupon this Lease and the term hereof shall automatically (without any further action on the part of either party) cease, determine and terminate, and it shall then be lawful for Landlord, at Landlord's option, to re-enter the Leased Premises without further demand of rent or demand of possession thereof and recover possession thereof by whatever process of law may be available in the jurisdiction in which the Leased Premises are located, any notice to quit or of intention to re-enter being hereby expressly waived by Tenant, or Landlord may re-take possession without process of law. In the event of such re-entry or re-taking, Tenant shall nevertheless remain liable and answerable for the full rental to the date of such re-taking or re-entry, and for damages for the deficiency or loss of rent which Landlord may thereby sustain in respect of the balance of the term of this Lease; and in such case, Landlord shall have the right to alter and/or repair the Leased Premises (at Tenant's expense) and let the same for the benefit of Tenant, in liquidation and discharge, in whole or in part, as the case may be, of the liability of Tenant hereunder; and such damages at the option of Landlord may be recovered at the time of the re-taking or re-entry, or in separate actions from time to time as Tenant's obligation to pay rent would have accrued if the term of this Lease had continued, or from time to time as said damages shall have been made more easily ascertainable by re-lettings, or such action, at the option of Landlord, may be deferred until the expiration of the term of this Lease, in which latter event, the cause of action shall not be deemed to have accrued until the expiration of said term. Landlord, however, may refrain from terminating Tenant's right of possession, and in such case, may enforce against Tenant the provisions of the Lease for the full term hereof. In the event legal proceedings are instituted against Tenant by Landlord, either for payment of rent or for possession, then Tenant agrees to pay all costs and expenses incident to such proceedings, including,but not limited to, reasonable attorney's fees.

14. Subordination.

This Lease is subject and subordinate to the lien of any mortgage, deed of trust or other encumbrance now or at any time hereafter placed upon the Leased Premises or any part thereof, and Tenant hereby agrees to execute and deliver any and all instruments or documents which Landlord may request or require to evidence or effectuate such subordination.

15. Quiet Enjoyment.

Landlord covenants and warrants to Tenant that it is the owner in fee simple of the Leased Premises and has the full right to enter into this Lease. Landlord covenants and agrees that so long as Tenant continues to perform its obligations hereunder, Tenant shall have continuous, peaceful, uninterrupted and exclusive possession and quiet enjoyment of the Leased Premises during the term of this Lease, subject to compliance with the terms hereof. Tenant also agrees to cease any activity that would prevent other Tenants from enjoying their right to quiet enjoyment.

16. Tenant's Liability and Indemnification of Landlord.

16.1 The operation of Tenant's business, and all persons and personal property in or on the Leased Premises shall be at the risk and the responsibility of Tenant. Landlord shall not be liable for any loss, damage or injury to said business, persons or personal property arising from floods, storms or other natural causes, the negligence or acts or omissions of Tenant, leaks, the freezing, bursting, leaking or overflowing of water, steam, sewer or gas pipes, heating or plumbing fixtures, electric wires or fixtures, or from or by any other cause whatsoever, latent or patent. In summary, Landlord shall not be liable for any injury or damage whatever to the business, person or property of Tenant or any other person or entity in or on the Leased Premises.

16.2 Tenant will defend against and will hold Landlord harmless and indemnify Landlord from and against any and all claims, suits, damages, expenses or causes of action, including attorneys' fees, relating to any claim brought from damages resulting from any injury to persons or property or loss of life sustained in or about the Leased Premises during the term hereof.

17. Inspection.

Landlord and Landlord's agents and representatives shall have the right to enter upon the Leased Premises at reasonable times for the purpose of inspecting, repairing or maintaining the Leased Premises and exhibiting it to prospective purchasers, mortgagees and/or tenants, and, for a period of six (6) months prior to the expiration of this Lease, Landlord and Landlord's agents or representatives may place signs on the Leased Premises indicating that the Leased Premises are "For Sale" or "For Rent" and the person to contact in connection therewith; such signs to be erected in such manner as not to interfere with the operation of Tenant's business.

18. Waiver.

No waiver or oversight of any breach of any covenant, condition or agreement herein contained, or compromise or settlement relating to such a breach, shall operate as a waiver of the covenant, condition or agreement itself, or of any subsequent breach thereof.

19. Holding Over.

In the event Tenant continues to occupy the Leased Premises after the last day of the term hereby created or after any extension or renewal thereof, and Landlord elects to accept rent thereafter, a tenancy from month to month shall be created.

20. Notices.

20.1 All notices required to be given to Tenant hereunder shall be deemed sufficiently given if personally delivered by Landlord or Landlord's agents, or sent by registered or certified mail, return receipt requested, first class, postage prepaid, addressed to Tenant at the Leased Premises, or to such other address as Tenant shall hereafter designate by written Notice to Landlord.

20.2 All notices required to be given to Landlord hereunder shall be deemed sufficiently given if personally delivered or sent by registered or certified mail, return receipt requested, first class postage prepaid, addressed to Landlord at _____, or to such other address as Landlord shall hereafter designate in writing.

20.3 Any such notice shall be deemed to have been duly given when personally delivered to Tenant or to Tenant's mail receiving box at the address of the Leased Premises, or when enclosed in a properly sealed envelope and deposited in the mails as aforesaid.

21. Entire Understanding.

This lease constitutes the entire understanding between the parties. It is understood that the signature page may be in duplicate in order to accommodate the signature of the co-signer. No representations except as herein expressly set forth have been made by either party to the other party, and this Lease cannot be modified or cancelled except pursuant to a written instrument duly executed and delivered by Landlord and Tenant.

IN WITNESS THEREOF, and intending to be legally bound, Landlord and Tenant, having authority to do so, have duly executed this Lease Agreement under seal on this day and year so indicated below.

(LANDLORD)

By:

_____Date _____
By: (printed name) ,
with authority to sign for the (corporate name)

(TENANT)

_____ Date _____
(Name), personally
Address
Telephone number
Social Security or Federal ID number

Sample Cover Letter:

Name of the building owner/corporation/partnership:
Address

Date

Tenant:

Re: Studio Unit _____

Dear _____:

    I am enclosing two commercial leases for Studio _____ for you to read. Please sign both of them and return them to me together with your payment of $_____.00, representing the first and last month's rent. (A certified check is needed for the first payment in order to activate this lease.) When I receive this material, I will sign both leases and return one signed copy to you.

    Checks should be made out to "_____." After this payment, rent by regular check is normally sent to the address above by the first of the month. Your next payment will be due _____.

    The studio is "as is." The rent is $_____per month, starting ____(date)____. You must contact the electric company immediately to have the electrical account put into your name effective at the first of the month.

    Call me if you have any questions. I hope you enjoy your studio and the other artists in the building.

Very truly yours,

Enclosed: 2 leases

Index

accounting 190
architects 116
artists' buildings 205, 213
artists' committees...............................205
artists' not-for-profit facilities 218
artists' organizations 205
asbestos 77, 148
bank financing 89
bartering...83
bathrooms 175, 200
Beaver Mill......................................13,34
bedroom, guest 199
bedroom...198
bricks, exposed 144
Brown, Diane 23
building codes 73, 150
cable, TV and internet...........................173
Carter, Stevens 131
ceilings...143
Clark Art Institute 45
cleaning 123
closing costs 76
commercial condominium.......................91
concrete 160
conduit..136, 161
construction 121
Contemporary Artists Center.....................
..................................93, 146, 214, 220
Cornell, Joseph 30
corporations..96
Cor-x 141, 159
cost of living 44
cost per square foot 51
credit cards 193
Damos, Betsy 193
Dark Ride Project 214
designing 109
DIA Foundation.............................37, 221
Diane Brown Gallery 23
display space 174
drywall...163

ductwork 161
electric rates...180
electrical, systems 136
electrical, wire 136
electrical rates 180
elevator 146
emergency systems 151
energy programs 190
estate planning.......................................222
exhibition galleries 217
financing 88
firewalls...151
flexible hose 167
floors 144, 157
Foundation, The Judith
    Rothschild 223
Foundation, The Marie
    Walsh Sharpe Art................................223
furniture...201
Geldzahler, Henry 23
Haffner, Andrea 175
handicapped access 151
hazardous wastes.............................77, 147
heating and air conditioning 131
historic designation 74
inspections.......................................72, 125
insulation 129
insurance 76, 184
intercoms 168
internet..173
Judd, Don 21, 37, 221
keys 183
Kiefer, Anslem...21
Kienholz, Ed 16
kitchenettes 175
kitchens 197
labor...152, 209
lead paint 148
leases 56, 98
leasing 48
legal, contracts.......................................95

legal, leases 56, 98
legal, tenant issues..................189
Lexan, GE Plastics 140
light, natural 167
lighting 137, 162
loading docks.........................170
location 43
location 196
lofts, accessory use 195
Louis, Morris..........................28
mail systems 168
maintenance, heating..................181
maintenance, plumbing 181
maintenance, supplies 187
maintenance, water and sewer.........183
Marfa, Texas 37, 221
MASS MoCA_ 26, 159, 162, 215
mills..................................31
mortgage amortization.................85
negotiation............................63
neighborhoods 43
new construction 19
New York City studios 21,31
North Adams, MA.......................32
office station 173
open studios..........................207
operational expenses 179
paint.............................145, 158
paint, spraying 145
painting walls 144
parking lots 147
parties 208
partitions 115
partnerships......................91, 96
payroll systems 190
PCBs 77
plants 168
plastic sheeting 157
plexiglas..............................141
plumbing 139
Pollock, Jackson 28
polyurethane foam.....................160
public goals 224

public use............................74
purchase contract.....................65
purchasing 59, 85
Rauschenberg, Robert 34
rent, collecting.......................191
repairs, emergency....................182
residency codes 195
residency facilities...................212
roofs.................................127
room, dining 200
room, living..........................200
safety................................126
security 142, 192, 208
sheetrock 163
shelving 166
Smith, David 16, 33
snow removal 187
SoHo lofts 31
sole proprietor 96
sprinkler systems 134,
structural 128
studio, drawing 172
studio, painting 172
studio, print 172
taxes, real-estate 186
taxes.................................97
telephone 173, 184
tenants, problems....................106
tenants, screening 206
theater groups 211
tools 169
trash 182
utilities 77
Voulkos, Peter 21
wallboard............................163
walls 143, 164
Warhol, Andy.........................21
water heaters 183
Williams College Museum of Art 45
window shades 163
windows..............................140
woodshop.............................171
zoning 75

asy Order Form

orders: (413) 663-6662 (Send this form)
phone orders: Call (800) 689-0978 toll free

/e your credit card ready.)
ne orders available at www.cirecorp.com

al orders: Cire Corporaton - Publisher
oric Beaver Mill, 189 Beaver Street, North Adams, MA 01247-2873. USA.

se send the following books: I understand that I may return any of them for a full
nd, for any reason, no questions asked.

E ART WORLD DREAM
rnative Strategies for Working Artists by Eric Rudd

E STUDIO/LOFT MANUAL
Ambitious Artists and Creators by Eric Rudd

ntity _____ THE ART WORLD DREAM @ $19.95   Total: $_____
ntity _____THE ART STUDIO/LOFT MANUAL @ $19.95   Total: $_____
                TOTAL FOR BOOKS: $_____
                Massachusetts Residents Add 5% $_____
                Shipping $_____
                Total Enclosed or Charged: $_____

ping by air: US: $4 for the first book and $2 for each additional book.
rnational: $9 for the first book and $5 for each additional book.

nod of payment: ❑ Check   ❑ Money Order   ❑ Credit Card
nent: Check or Money Order payable to Cire Corp in the amount of: $ _____
lit Card: ❑ Visa   ❑ Mastercard   ❑ AmEx
d number _____
e on Card_____   Exp. Date: _____/_____
ature _____

:haser -ship to:
ne: _____
ress:_____
_____State _____ Zip: _____
phone:_____
til address:_____

book is a gift, enclose a card that says a gift from: _____
ship the book to the name and address below:
• to Gift Recipient: (if blank, we will ship to purchaser)
ne: _____
ress:_____
_____State _____ Zip: _____
phone:_____
til address:_____

lease have someone contact me about speaking/seminars
ne and address of Institution or Organization: _____
_____

asy Order Form

CORPORATION
P U B L I S H E R

orders: (413) 663-6662 (Send this form)
ohone orders: Call (800) 689-0978 toll free

e your credit card ready.)
ne orders available at www.cirecorp.com

al orders: Cire Corporaton - Publisher
oric Beaver Mill, 189 Beaver Street, North Adams, MA 01247-2873. USA.

se send the following books: I understand that I may return any of them for a full
nd, for any reason, no questions asked.

E ART WORLD DREAM
native Strategies for Working Artists by Eric Rudd

E STUDIO/LOFT MANUAL
Ambitious Artists and Creators by Eric Rudd

ntity _____ THE ART WORLD DREAM @	$19.95	Total:	$_____
ntity _____THE ART STUDIO/LOFT MANUAL @ $19.95		Total:	$_____
TOTAL FOR BOOKS:			$_____
Massachusetts Residents Add 5%			$_____
Shipping			$_____
Total Enclosed or Charged:			$_____

oing by air: US: $4 for the first book and $2 for each additional book.
national: $9 for the first book and $5 for each additional book.

od of payment: ❏ Check   ❏ Money Order   ❏ Credit Card
ient: Check or Money Order payable to Cire Corp in the amount of: $ _____
it Card: ❏ Visa   ❏ Mastercard   ❏ AmEx
 number _____
e on Card_____   Exp. Date: _____/_____
ature _____

naser -ship to:
e: _____
ess: _____
_____State _____ Zip: _____
hone:_____
l address:_____

oook is a gift, enclose a card that says a gift from: _____
ship the book to the name and address below:
to Gift Recipient: (if blank, we will ship to purchaser)
e: _____
ess: _____
_____State _____ Zip: _____
hone:_____
l address:_____

ease have someone contact me about speaking/seminars
 and address of Institution or Organization: _____

asy Order Form

orders: (413) 663-6662 (Send this form)
ephone orders: Call (800) 689-0978 toll free

ve your credit card ready.)
ine orders available at www.cirecorp.com

tal orders: Cire Corporaton - Publisher
toric Beaver Mill, 189 Beaver Street, North Adams, MA 01247-2873. USA.

ase send the following books: I understand that I may return any of them for a full
nd, for any reason, no questions asked.

E ART WORLD DREAM
rnative Strategies for Working Artists by Eric Rudd

E STUDIO/LOFT MANUAL
Ambitious Artists and Creators by Eric Rudd

antity _____ THE ART WORLD DREAM @	$19.95	Total:	$_____
antity _____THE ART STUDIO/LOFT MANUAL @ $19.95		Total:	$_____
	TOTAL FOR BOOKS:		$
	Massachusetts Residents Add 5%		$_____
	Shipping		$_____
	Total Enclosed or Charged:		$_____

pping by air: US: $4 for the first book and $2 for each additional book.
rnational: $9 for the first book and $5 for each additional book.

hod of payment: ❑ Check   ❑ Money Order   ❑ Credit Card
ment: Check or Money Order payable to Cire Corp in the amount of: $ _____
dit Card: ❑ Visa   ❑ Mastercard   ❑ AmEx
d number _____
ne on Card_____   Exp. Date: _____/_____
nature _____

chaser -ship to:
ne: _____
ress: _____
_____State _____ Zip: _____
phone:_____
ail address:_____

book is a gift, enclose a card that says a gift from: _____
ship the book to the name and address below:
to Gift Recipient: (if blank, we will ship to purchaser)
ne: _____
ress: _____
_____State _____ Zip: _____
phone:_____
ail address:_____

lease have someone contact me about speaking/seminars
ne and address of Institution or Organization: _____
_____